Social Marketing for Business

Mark Sarner & **Janice Nathanson**

Edited by **Tim Hurson**

Manifest Communications Inc.

117 Peter Street, Toronto, Ontario, Canada M5V 2G9 • Tel: 416.593.7017 • email ideas@manifestcom.com

Sarner, Mark and Janice Nathanson
   Social Marketing for Business

   Includes bibliographical references
   ISBN 0-9680-334-0-7
   1. Social Marketing for Business
   I. Sarner, Mark and Janice Nathanson
   II. Title

Published by Manifest Communications Inc.
117 Peter Street, Toronto, Ontario
Canada   M5V 2G9

email   ideas@manifestcom.com

To our clients.

PREFACE

Why is social change suddenly of such vital interest to business? Since when has doing well become a benefit of doing good?

More and more, companies are asking these questions — and looking for answers. No, they have not lost touch with reality. Rather, they are trying to adapt to a new one, a marketplace where corporate values and social action are increasingly central to business success. The corporate sector is re-thinking and re-tooling its approach to social issues. Companies are searching for ways and means to make their new social activism pay off — in terms of positive social change and a healthier bottom line. Just some of the returns businesses are looking for include increased sales, an enhanced corporate image, stronger brand equity, better employee relations, and improved consumer and stakeholder relations.

It is in this context that social marketing has become of compelling interest to business. This handbook is designed to meet the growing demand from the corporate sector for a better understanding of social marketing and for practical advice on how to use it as a means of securing competitive advantage in today's marketplace.

Our goal is to provide perspective, insight, and useful advice on how best to meld a social agenda with core business strategy. Effectively. Efficiently. Appropriately. Productively. To do so, there are things you need to know and things you need to do. Both areas are covered in this handbook.

Properly applied, social marketing can deliver on the dual promise of making the world a better place and the company a healthy return. Some of the pioneers, The Body Shop, Becel Margarine, Nike, and Imperial Oil among them, are part of a new kind of social activism — a corporate movement that *Harvard Business Review* has called the fastest growing trend in marketing today.

Before you can effectively use this powerful marketing tool, however, a few words of caution are in order. At first glance, it all looks straight-forward. Master the buzzwords, pick an issue that looks hot, and run with it. Unfortunately, it isn't quite that simple. Those who try to use social marketing for business as a quick fix to long-term problems, as a one-time effort to get quick returns, or as a cover-up for improper behaviour, are

Properly applied, social marketing can deliver on the dual promise of making the world a better place and the company a healthy return.

i

going to fail. Those who make a token commitment to the process can expect a token response from the market.

A New Approach to an Old Idea

Contributing to the social good isn't a new idea to business. Philanthropy is part of a well-established business tradition: Do business; make money; give some of it back to the community by responding to requests from charitable organizations. The tradition endures; in fact, evidence shows that corporate donations in Canada are on the rise. There is, however, a major change taking place in how corporate philanthropy is practised — and who within the corporation is responsible for it.

Today's sense of social responsibility no longer measures the number of causes to which the company gives time and money. Nor is it confined to the work of the corporate donations office or the charitable acts of senior executives. Corporations are no longer content to simply write cheques or lend their names to good causes. Rather, social activism has become an increasingly important component of corporate and marketing strategies that target consumers, the trade, regulators, and employees alike.

Social Marketing for Business

The appeal of social marketing to business is its potential to help companies achieve their social and business goals.

The formal relationship between marketing and social change began nearly sixty years ago with the question: "Why can't we sell brotherhood the way we sell soap?". At the time, marketers were imbued with the evangelical belief that marketing could work miracles in shaping human behaviour.

After a few decades of trying to answer that seminal question, two things became clear. First, you can't sell brotherhood in the same way you sell soap; second, marketing does have a great deal to offer the social change process. In 1971, the application of marketing principles and practices to social change was legitimized by famed marketing professor, Dr. Philip Kotler, of Northwestern University. Kotler, along with his colleague Gerald Zaltman, gave the field name — social marketing — and its first definition. Kotler's premise was that non-profit organizations could increase their influence on social change by adopting and adapting a marketing orientation to their work. In short, business could teach social change agents a thing or two.

Today's sense of social responsibility no longer measures the number of causes to which the company gives time and money.

Twenty-five years later, things have come full circle. Social marketing has demonstrated its capacity for influencing social change. Now, it is offering business a methodology for achieving greater success in the marketplace. The move by business to social marketing is clearly under way. The question now is: "How can you sell soap *by* selling brotherhood?". The answer? By adopting and adapting the principles and practices of social marketing to core business strategy.

The question now is: "How can you sell soap by selling brotherhood?".

Since 1981, Manifest Communications has been helping organizations do exactly that. Our corporate mission is "To help our clients become effective agents of positive change." Our success is a function of both the social change our clients foster and the benefits that accrue to them in terms of image, influence, and income. If experience is the best teacher, we've received an excellent social marketing education. Over the last decade and a half, we've had the opportunity to apply social marketing to the major issues confronting Canadians. From aging to AIDS, from the environment to employment equity, heart health, dental health, mental health, substance abuse, spousal abuse. . . the list goes on. In each case, the challenge has been to find the most effective means of translating our client's social change agenda into positive social action.

The single most important lesson we have learned along the way is the need for a thorough, informed, and disciplined approach to the process of fostering and sustaining social change. We've used this hard-won knowledge as the basis for this handbook. For the purposes of illustration, we've included real examples of how corporations have addressed their own social marketing challenges. The result is, we hope, an illuminating and practical guide to help business develop an effective social marketing orientation.

From Principles to Practice
A marketing orientation is a prerequisite for using this handbook. We won't be spending any time on commercial marketing theory or on a review of standard marketing terms or techniques. We assume that if you are in business today, you are already more than up to speed.

Nor do we spend much time on social marketing theory or history. For those who are interested there are a number of books to read, a growing number of articles being published, and an ongoing academic debate to monitor and join.

This handbook is for practitioners with an urgent need to find out what they need to know and what they need to do to be successful in Social Marketing for Business. And there's a lot to know and do.

- You'll have to gain a fresh understanding of target markets and publics — one that focuses on their attitudes towards the world around them and their role in it; their deepest hopes, concerns, values, and beliefs.

- You'll have to figure how to satisfy a new set of wants and needs — not what people want and need from a product, but what they want and need from the world and from themselves.

- You'll have to learn how to harness ideas for their social impact rather than for their consumer appeal — to brand ideas and package them in ways that are distinctive for their power and influence.

- You'll have to develop new partnerships with non-profits and government that enable you to work with them — instead of around or in spite of them.

- You'll have to find ways to strengthen relationships with your markets based not only on the added value you bring to your products and services, but the added values you demonstrate in your work in the world.

- And, you'll have to redefine your measures of success to include not just share of market and pocketbook, but also share of heart and mind.

As we said, there's a lot to cover. We take you through it step-by-step. Our starting point is to help you determine whether or not social marketing has any relevance to your business. From there, we provide a grounding in social marketing and an overview of the forces that are motivating more and more businesses to make social marketing an integral part of their business strategy.

Seven practical principles provide the framework for approaching social marketing in a business context. Checklists, charts, glossaries and summaries of issues and ideas combine to enable you to translate knowledge into action as quickly as possible. In the end, you will have an informed perspective on the issues and challenges ahead, and an inventory of tools and techniques to help you address them head-on.

This handbook is for practitioners with an urgent need to find out what they need to know and what they need to do to be successful in Social Marketing for Business.

How to Use This Book

There is no one way to use this book. Your approach to it should probably be driven by where you are in terms of your business's relationship to social change and in terms of your professional responsibilities.

If you are in corporate public affairs, use it as an aid to re-evaluating how a social marketing program might have a positive impact on corporate image, and stakeholder and government relations.

If you are in corporate or brand marketing, use it as a guide to understanding the tidal wave of interest in cause and social marketing as a means of building brand image and market share.

If you are a senior executive, use it as a primer on how your company can gain greater profile, power, and influence in the public policy and community arenas. Discover how social marketing can help you galvanize your employees by giving new meaning to their sense of common cause and new resolve to their sense of common purpose.

If you are from the non-profit or government sector, use it to gain a working understanding of how corporations will address social issues in the future.

If you are starting from scratch, work your way right through all seven principles. But if you're not at square one — and many companies aren't — use this handbook as a kind of operator's manual. Look up what interests you or what you need to deal with right now and work from there.

In principle, this process, like many others, is intended to be logical and sequential; in practice, it tends not to be quite so linear. There's a good chance you'll be revisiting key issues and related principles several times as you work towards the development and execution of your program. You can start almost anywhere as long as you ensure that steps aren't skipped and elements are not overlooked.

When all is said and done, social marketing is an orientation to achieving business goals and social objectives. Success is a function of how well you apply the principles of social marketing to your business challenges. Good luck!

Seven practical principles provide the framework for approaching social marketing in a business context.

CONTENTS

IS SOCIAL MARKETING FOR YOU?

An introduction

Nike. The Body Shop. Labatt Breweries. Imperial Oil. These are just some of the companies at the forefront of the fastest growing trend in corporate marketing today — Social Marketing for Business (SMB). It's a new way of thinking about building brand equity, corporate image, and competitive advantage, while contributing to society at the same time.

Social Marketing and Business

Social Marketing for Business is a strategic and programmatic approach to harnessing a social agenda to business strategy. In essence, SMB is the effort put forth by companies to add a social change dimension to their business and corporate objectives.

Social Marketing for Business was born out of social marketing, a discipline that has been around since 1971. Philip Kotler coined the term and defined it as "the design, implementation, and control of programs calculated to influence the acceptability of social ideas and involving considerations of product planning, pricing, communication, distribution, and market research." While the definition is academic, one compelling point is clear: The social change process is based on a marketing orientation.

Social marketing is a planned process for fostering societal change by influencing people's attitudes, understanding, and behaviour. The discipline is based upon the principles and techniques that underlie the marketing of commercial products and services, adapted to a different marketplace, and to the promotion of different commodities.

Why Now?

Until recently, social marketing has been used primarily by government and non-profit organizations. Now business is turning to SMB in search of an innovative and sustained approach to achieving social and business objectives. Many companies have come to realize that doing well can be a direct result of doing good. A number of forces combine to drive corporate thinking to that conclusion:

"Social Marketing for Business is an industry that is hovering around the one billion dollar mark in the United States."

Customer Bonding: Pathway to Lasting Customer Loyalty

The overriding goal of Social Marketing for Business is to create long-term, sustained programming that is central to business objectives and corporate values. SMB provides a methodology for companies to establish social change objectives, understand their options, plan their programs, allocate their resources, and choose the issues and partners that are right for them.

1) There is a new kind of consumer

The smarter, more discerning, more socially aware Canadian consumers of the '90s are expecting companies to make a difference. In a survey called *Market Vision 2000*, 94 per cent of respondents said they would rather do business with a "good" company than a "bad" one. Ninety per cent said it's inadequate to only provide well-priced, quality products or services — that's merely the cost of entry into today's game of business. *Market Vision* further reported that, in 1993, 26 per cent of Canadians — or 5.5 million people — boycotted companies for what they considered to be unacceptable corporate practices: poor labour relations, abuse of animals, environmental neglect, and the like. According to a 1991 report by Decima Research, Canadians do not believe that companies should be motivated solely by altruism. The study finds, for example, that regardless of industries' motives, the public wants to see environmentally friendly companies rewarded by tax breaks. Overwhelmingly, the public views this type of activity pragmatically — as smart business. As the Decima study states, "Good morals is good marketing is good business."

*"Good morals is
good marketing is
good business."*

Decima Research

2) The marketplace has changed

It is becoming increasingly difficult to maintain competitive advantage based on product attributes or service innovation. Today, products and services are becoming increasingly generic. Quality, price, taste, and innovation aren't working the way they used to. Where consumers once demanded added value, now they're looking for added values.

According to the *Market Vision* study, "even the strongest, brand-lead industries achieve no higher than a 4.51 score on a seven-point product/service differentiation scale." Industries in the most serious trouble when it comes to consumers distinguishing their products or services include pharmaceuticals, life insurance, brewing, banking and trust, and oil and gas.

3) There are increased demands from the charitable sector

Corporations are faced with a staggering number of requests, but don't have enough money to satisfy the range of charities and non-profits that need help. Federal Express says it averages 30 solicitations each week from fund-raisers. According to the *Corporate Ethics Monitor*, Chrysler Canada receives an average of 2,000 requests annually for philanthropic support. Public affairs and donations offices of major

SOCIAL MARKETING FOR BUSINESS: WHAT IT'S NOT

IT'S NOT A COVER-UP

If you're looking for some good PR to get you out of a bad situation, don't look to social marketing. Today's consumer is too sophisticated and skeptical to be snowed.

IT'S NOT THE SWEEPSTAKES

Social Marketing for Business is not a quick fix for long-term problems. Don't use it the same way you would a sales promotion, or a one-time event sponsorship to get quick returns. For SMB to be effective, it has to be sustained.

IT'S NOT CHARITY

Social Marketing for Business is not simply another name for philanthropy. Rather, SMB focuses on the bottom-line impact of doing good. It is a programmatic commitment to hands-on social problem solving in a manner that brings measurable returns to the corporation itself.

corporations are inundated with requests for help. Companies are realizing that they can have greater impact by aligning themselves with one or two issues rather than by giving a few dollars to many groups.

4) The old reliables aren't reliable any more

Corporations are looking for new ways of winning the marketing war. The old reliables simply aren't reliable any more. Advertising, public relations, direct mail, and other traditional vehicles aren't generating the returns they once did. There are too many messages, too much mail, too many events, and too much competition for the consumer to cut through the clutter. In accepting the 1995 Sales and Marketing Executives International Excellence in Marketing Award, Bruce Pope, then President of Molson Breweries, said "The time-honoured formula of selling beer with product, packaging, and advertising is insufficient for building brands today. We are now building brands through new media, value-laden messages, and two-way dialogue with our customers."

5) The public sector is more demanding than ever

Corporations are now more accountable to government and to public opinion. In terms of government, a good brief and good contacts are not enough to win the day. In the public domain, consumer advocates and special interest groups command more attention and profile than ever before. Whether the threat of censure is explicit or implicit, companies are now realizing that their every action is being watched. A company's ability to conduct business will invariably be affected by its perceived social behaviour.

Is It for You?

You need a compelling reason to make social marketing an integral part of your business strategy. In general, there are three motivating factors that could propel you into the social change business.

Reason #1. There's a problem. The problem may be a crisis, such as a human or environmental catastrophe (the Exxon Valdez oil spill or Union Carbide and Bhopal or Tylenol's tainted capsules). The problem may be less visible and volatile, such as impending legislation or regulation. The problem may simply be bad press or angered interest groups in response to your employment equity policies. It may be that

According to the 1994 Cone/Roper Benchmark Survey, 78 per cent of consumers surveyed said they would be more likely to buy a product that is associated with a cause they care about.

Is SMB for You? A Relevance Test

*Social Marketing for Business isn't the solution to every business
dilemma. It does, however, offer a fresh and workable approach to a
variety of problems.*

*Here is a quick relevance test to help you decide if social marketing
is for you. Read each statement below. If it applies to your situation,
check it off.*

☐   1.   *I've got an image problem, either corporately or with a
particular brand.*

☐   2.   *My company is in an industry in which most products or
services are generic.*

☐   3.   *Traditional marketing tools aren't bringing the returns
they once did.*

☐   4.   *Regulatory issues are becoming increasingly threatening.*

☐   5.   *My sales force is losing heat.*

☐   6.   *Morale and productivity are low.*

☐   7.   *I'm losing market share.*

☐   8.   *It's harder and harder to build and maintain brand loyalty.*

☐   9.   *I can't win a price war.*

☐   10.   *The "me-too" brands are encroaching on my territory.*

*If you checked off any of these statements, keep reading. You'll probably
find SMB both relevant and valuable.*

you're pulling out of a community in which you are the major employer. Or the problem may be one that is not crisis or issue-related. For example, you may be faced with a sluggish and demoralized work force, declining sales, or diminishing brand loyalty. Whatever the problem, smart companies respond not merely with apologies or defences, but with a proactive initiative to demonstrate that the corporation is, indeed, committed to the right issues.

This in no way implies that a company can cause severe environmental damage or tolerate racism and cover up its bad behaviour with good PR. This approach is not only unpalatable and unethical, it also won't work. If your problem is a crisis, what you need is expert crisis management and public relations. Once the immediate catastrophe has ended, you'll likely be left with another kind of crisis — a breakdown in consumer confidence and an erosion of your relationship with your markets. This is where you can start thinking long-term about a response to real issues with real programming that contributes to real change — in other words, Social Marketing for Business.

Reason #2. Opportunity is knocking. Companies use social marketing because they want to seize an opportunity. For example, they may want to establish more meaningful relationships with their customers. This is no different than any other effort to gain ground through traditional marketing activity. Becel Margarine, for instance, has based its entire marketing strategy on the promotion of heart health. For its part, Eli Lilly, manufacturer of Prozac, has teamed up with the Canadian Mental Health Association in an extensive social marketing program to promote understanding of the signs and symptoms of depression. There may be direct business opportunities as well. American Express supports arts and entertainment as a vehicle for increasing consumer use of its credit cards.

Reason #3. There are certain industries that have little choice. Companies, particularly those in regulated industries, are increasingly under pressure to demonstrate their social value in return for the privilege of operating in a controlled marketplace. Think oil, banks, energy, telecommunications. The alcohol industry is especially vulnerable. Perceived as the purveyor of substances that may be a threat to the public's health and safety, manufacturers must demonstrate that they are not driven by profit at the expense of people. Labatt Breweries' *Know When to Draw the Line* campaign, for

"Competing on price and corporate citizenship is a smarter strategy than competing on price alone."

Harvard Business Review

Philanthropic and business units have joined forces to develop giving strategies that increase their name recognition among consumers, boost employee productivity, reduce R&D costs, overcome regulatory obstacles and foster synergy among business units... This new paradigm encourages corporations to play a leadership role in social problem solving by funding long-term initiatives like school reform and AIDS awareness that incorporate the best thinking of non-profits and government institutions.

Harvard Business Review

example, has demonstrated to government, special interest groups, the media, and the public alike a sincere and sustained commitment to promoting the responsible use of alcohol.

SMB offers answers to many of the major challenges that corporations face today. As with any methodology, however, success is a function of the precise application of sound thinking and the strategic execution of tactics. In other words, program effectiveness is dependent upon what you know and how you translate that knowledge into action.

Program effectiveness is dependent upon what you know and how you translate that knowledge into action.

This handbook is designed to help. It provides an organized approach to planning a Social Marketing for Business program built on seven principles:

RELEVANCE IS EVERYTHING: Choosing Your Issues

RESULTS COME OVER TIME, NOT OVERNIGHT: Defining Success

HEARTS AND MINDS RULE POCKETBOOKS: Targeting Your Audiences

ONE PLUS ONE EQUALS THREE: Establishing Partnerships

BRAND IT!: Positioning The Issue

MAKE CHANGE, NOT NOISE: Developing Your Program

THE MAP IS NOT THE TERRITORY: Turning Strategy Into Action

CHOOSING YOUR ISSUES

Relevance is everything

It's hard enough doing business in the commercial marketplace. Today you find yourself working in another arena as well — the Marketplace of Ideas. The stakes are huge. As Victor Hugo said, "More powerful than all the armies in the world is an idea whose time has come." Ideas have the capacity to reshape the world, and everyone in it — including business and industry.

There isn't a single industry that isn't affected by social change. Corporations can no longer escape the intensive scrutiny of policy-makers and special interest groups. If you're in the food industry, you're in the health management business. If you're in cosmetics, you're in the ethical testing business. And if you cater to kids, you'd better be working in their interests. Even your employees are demanding more. They want to work for a company that shares their values, expresses their concerns, and addresses the issues that matter to them.

In short, whether you like it or not, you're in the social change business. But how and to what end? Most companies are on the wrong side of the process — they are not agents of change, but targets of it. That's risky business. It's an opportunity missed, not only on the doing-good ledger, but for the bottom line.

How do you decide what issues are right for you? It's a process. Do your research. Consider your options. Evaluate and prioritize your markets, the ones that matter most to you, and the ones with whom you need to establish meaningful relationships and build loyalty. Base your choice not on what's most popular to most Canadians, but on what's most relevant to your markets, employees, sales force, shareholders, and other key stakeholders.

Most companies are on the wrong side of the process — they are not agents of change, but victims of it.

What to Know

Here are the criteria for choosing an issue:

Who Cares?
The bottom line is relevance. Choose an issue your markets care about. Some choices are more obvious than others. No nonsense Pantyhose is a case in point. The brand's core marketing strategy is to celebrate the contribution of women to society. Through its multi-faceted campaign, No nonsense presents individual women with a BIO award each month

What to Avoid

☛ **THE TOP-DOWN SYNDROME:** *The days are long gone when CEOs could pick corporate causes based solely on their own personal interests and priorities. A corporate social agenda should be created based on what's best for the business.*

☛ **THE BANDWAGON:** *Just because the environment and AIDS are high on the public's agenda, and just because a lot of corporations are addressing these issues, that doesn't mean they're right for you. You should align yourself with an issue that's relevant to your markets, and that distinguishes your company from the competition.*

☛ **THE KNEE-JERK REACTION:** *Choosing an issue while you're under the gun is no way to ensure a sound decision. It takes time — and research — to choose the issue or cause that's right for your organization. Don't fight fires.*

☛ **"THE ISSUE OF THE MONTH":** *More isn't necessarily better. However good the campaign, the public can become cynical about a company that it perceives to be fickle when it comes to social action.*

to recognize their achievement and success. The program's aim is to strengthen and solidify the brand's relationship with markets by demonstrating a corporate commitment to women's issues and challenges.

Molson Breweries has chosen a bolder strategy. At first glance, it may appear that beer and AIDS make for strange bedfellows, but Molson is responding to the demographics, values, attitudes, opinions, and behaviours of its consumers. Study after study shows that AIDS ranks among the top areas of concern and priority for young adults, Molson's target market.

The bottom line is relevance. There's no use doing something your markets don't care about.

Who's Who?

Pick any issue and there's already an industry around it. Government, non-profit organizations, special interest groups, lobbyists, the media — they're all involved to some extent. You need to know who they are, and what they're doing. What are their positions on the issues? Are they allies or opponents? What programs have they put in place?

Neglect this investigation at your peril. According to media reports, Avon Canada took on the issue of breast cancer only to be met with stinging criticism surrounding the company's motives and priorities. Specifically, some non-profit organizations felt that Avon's issue focus was not appropriate, and that the company was not responding to the needs of breast cancer survivors. Avon did not sufficiently consider the issue marketplace it was entering; it didn't take into account the perspectives of other players.

What's What?

How long will an issue be around? Some issues come and go, getting extensive profile one day, only to be forgotten the next. The issue you choose should have sustained relevance to your markets.

You'll need to anticipate how your issue will affect your market at any given time. As with products, issues have a life cycle. They will affect markets differently at different times. For example, ten years from now the issue of AIDS for teenagers will likely be significantly different than it is today. Awareness and knowledge levels will be different. The way in which society has responded will influence perceptions, attitudes, and behaviors. People with AIDS may not be stigmatized the way they are today, and therefore, program messages, approaches, and tone may be entirely different in the next decade. What's important is

Tomorrow's successful company can no longer afford to be a faceless institution that does nothing more than sell the right product at the right price. It will have to present itself as a person — as an intelligent actor, of upright character, that brings explicit moral judgments to bear on its dealings with its employees and with the wider world.

Harvard Business Review

an understanding that what is effective with one group may not be effective with the same type of group even a short time later. The challenge is to ensure continued relevance by understanding where your issue and markets are — and where they are going.

Finally, consider the potential downside. Can the issues be turned against you? When the U.S.-based Christian Coalition asked AT&T to deny support to Planned Parenthood, the corporation conceded. In retaliation, Planned Parenthood took out a full-page advertisement in *The New York Times* to protest the action, which resulted in deep embarrassment to AT&T.

What's the Fit?

In searching for an issue, you may not have to look much further than your own line of business. American Express's sponsorship of a geography contest for students is relevant to the company's travel business. Bell Canada supports the Kids Help Phone, a toll-free line that puts troubled youth in touch with counsellors and social service agencies. Tele-Direct is helping to reduce illiteracy rates through advertisements in the Yellow Pages that refer people to organizations that can help them learn to read. And ASTRA Pharma Inc., a drug manufacturer, is committed to helping reduce health care costs in Canada through its *Sharing a Healthier Future* program.

But be careful. A tight fit with your line of business is not the only factor to consider when choosing your issue. Recent research (Drumwright, 1995) reveals that looser relationships between sponsor and cause tend to be most effective. Once again, Molson is a good example. While AIDS has little to do with the company's core business, the issue is extremely relevant to its consumers.

Drumwright says that, "Without a relationship between the company and an issue, dissonance may result...and key constituents, such as salespeople and retailers, may not develop an affinity for the cause." One example might be a packaged foods company that supports the opera; the relationship is so distant that personal relevance might not be perceived or understood. At the other extreme, consumers may be more cynical about a company's motive when there is a close relationship, because they perceive it to be "opportunistic or exploitative." An oil company and the environment is an example.

"Without a relationship between the company and an issue, dissonance may result. . . and key constituents, such as salespeople and retailers, may not develop an affinity for the cause."

M. Drumwright, 1995

The Top Five

Here's what Canadians rank highest on their issues agenda:

◆ *Job creation*

◆ *Crime prevention*

◆ *Affordable/accessible healthcare*

◆ *Environmental clean-up/protection*

◆ *Abuse of women*

Source: Market Vision 2000, 1993

16

What to Do

Look for a single social issue on which to focus your SMB program. The selection process involves the application of insight, judgement, and a bit of instinct based on sound knowledge.

Analyze the Market

Understanding your markets and publics is undoubtedly the most critical part of this exercise. Use all the information you have on the products and services side to build a consumer profile of your audiences, including demographics, psychographics, purchasing patterns and so forth. Then dig deeper. Look at the perceptions, attitudes, and behaviours of your markets in relation to key social issues. What concerns them? What affects them? What do they want and need to know more about? (We'll deal with market analysis in greater detail in "Targeting Your Audiences.")

Create a Short List

Select two or three social issues you think make sense for you, based on business and market needs. Articulate a clear rationale as to why you have chosen these for further consideration.

Audit the Issues

To figure out where you fit in, and where you can make the greatest difference corporately and socially, do an issues audit. Gather all relevant literature on the issue. Find the latest studies and surveys. Consult with relevant non-profit organizations and government agencies, and ask for their material. Review everything, keeping in mind that your task is to determine the nature of the issue, and what is currently being done to bring about change in relation to it.

Talk to experts about how they see the issue unfolding over the next year, the next three years, and the next decade. Look at issue prevalence, trends, and patterns. How long has the issue been of concern? Who is most concerned about it? Whom does it affect most? Who are its primary advocates? Opponents? Has its base of supporters changed over time? Likewise, has the positioning of the issue changed? How controversial is it?

A good fit with your line of business is not the only factor to consider when choosing your issue. Recent research reveals that looser relationships between sponsor and cause are the most effective.

Cause v. Effect

Social Marketing for Business is an approach to influencing the knowledge, attitudes, and behaviour of target audiences for social benefit and business advantage. There are a number of other terms floating around to describe how corporations are involving themselves in societal concerns. While these terms are often used interchangeably, they differ in intent and methodology. Here is a list of just some of these terms, along with working definitions.

Cause-Related Marketing (CRM): Attachment of a brand to a social issue for the dual purpose of sales promotion and fund-raising. CRM usually involves an offer to consumers through which their purchase will result in money going to a charity.

Marketing-Related Philanthropy: Strategic approach to the allocation of charitable dollars. Donation decisions are based on a fit with the corporate agenda and potential business benefits.

Issue Marketing: Promotion of a social cause or concern, usually for the purposes of influencing policy change. Issue marketing is a form of advocacy, usually focused on policy makers, gatekeepers, and stakeholders.

Don't forget to consider the issue's image. Some issues are just too controversial. Or too radical. Or too divisive. It's not sound judgement to hang your hat on an issue like abortion, unless you're absolutely sure where your markets stand in relation to it. For some companies, substance abuse is too sensitive an issue. For others, a global issue (such as international development) might make consumers wonder why the company's interests aren't local and community-based. Some issues are acceptable to virtually everyone — literacy is a good example (no one is *against* literacy). Most diseases are acceptable as well, especially those that concern children, such as juvenile diabetes. The downside to aligning yourself with such issues, however, is that issue ownership is extremely difficult because of the sheer number of corporate players who are already involved.

Assess the Marketplace

Find out who the other players are. Find out which corporations have already adopted the issue, and to what extent. Just because another company is already working in the area doesn't mean you can't. It just means you have to find your particular niche.

Choose the Author

Determine who the author, or sponsor, of the program should be. Is it your corporation, a product line, or a specific brand? Base your decision on business needs: a brand that is losing category share; a service that is primed to take off and is just waiting for the right launch; a better image as a corporate citizen.

Think about whether the author is credible in relation to your issue. It's probably imprudent for a rug importer to take on child labour issues in the Third World. Or for a soft drink company — often perceived to be part of the pollution problem — to take up the environment. Think about what you shouldn't be doing, as much as what you should. And of course, continued credibility is a function of doing what you say you're going to do. Think Body Shop. The company has made its name on its commitment to the environment and on its policy against animal testing. Suddenly, the media is filled with allegations that Body Shop suppliers test on animals. True or not, the image and credibility of the corporation has been brought into public question.

Just because another company is working in the area doesn't mean you can't. It just means you have to find your particular niche within the issue and figure out how to frame it distinctly.

In Review

Choosing Your Issues

WHAT TO KNOW

- **Who cares?**
  Know your markets
- **Who's who?**
  Know the social marketplace
- **What's what?**
  Know the issue
- **What's the fit?**
  Know your business

WHAT TO DO

- **Analyze the market**
  Do the research
- **Create a short list**
  Narrow it down to two or three
- **Audit the issues**
  Be comprehensive
- **Assess the marketplace**
  Look in all categories
- **Choose the author**
  Who's behind the program?
- **Choose the issue**
  Decide

Choose the Issue

By now you should have enough information to make an informed decision. Once you choose your issue, you should apply a rigorous process of objective setting, market identification, positioning, programming, and resource allocation. Keep reading for an understanding of how the process works.

DEFINING SUCCESS

Results come over time, not overnight

In SMB, as in all endeavors, the measure of success is the program's ability to meet the objectives set for it at the outset. In terms of social change objectives, you'll want to measure attitudes changed, knowledge shared, and behaviour redirected. Business motivations are invariably bottom-line: increased sales or market share; enhanced image; increased brand equity; higher productivity.

Realistic expectations are fundamental to SMB planning. Without them, programs are born in double jeopardy. On the one hand, they may be expected to work business miracles — to solve deeply entrenched problems overnight. On the other hand, SMB programs may have no clearly defined objectives. To make the situation even more difficult, these programs too often lack the commitment of time, attention or resources required to make a difference in either business or social terms.

Social marketing programs are only worth the effort if they are based on realistic objectives.

SMB programs are only worth the effort if they are based on realistic objectives. Their effectiveness can only be judged fairly against those objectives. These two statements are so basic it should be unnecessary to express them. Yet, a lack of defined expectations for success, often combined with a tendency to judge SMB against criteria not set for it in the first place, can lead to frustration and disappointment.

Your SMB program will need to define social and business objectives. Because the social and the business marketplaces are so different, you will have to understand what is reasonable in each. In the social arena, it is unrealistic to expect to "fix" complex problems in a single campaign. Similarly, your SMB initiative will not win back eroding market share or remake a tarnished brand or corporate image just like that.

The challenge in defining SMB success is not in how high you can set your sights, but in how grounded you can be in setting your course and measuring progress.

Examples of Business Objectives

◆ *Increase product/service sales*

◆ *Enhance customer loyalty*

◆ *Improve employee productivity*

◆ *Attract the best and the brightest employees*

◆ *Heighten employee morale*

◆ *Increase sales force/franchisee participation, satisfaction*

◆ *Enhance corporate image*

◆ *Improve regulatory affairs*

◆ *Improve trade response*

What to Know

The cornerstone of the SMB exercise is determining what you want your social marketing program to achieve. Here are some things to keep in mind, and some guidelines to help structure the objective setting process.

There Are Two Sets of Objectives

A social need is simply not enough to warrant the creation of a corporate social change program. Business objectives must drive the establishment of an SMB initiative. If a social cause is the primary impetus for programming, the result is often a marginalized effort, terminated once priorities change.

Nevertheless, once you do commit to an SMB program, it is essential that you establish social change objectives. There are two reasons. First, social change objectives are vital because you are staking part of your business success on your social success. Your company will be judged not only on its efforts, but on the results you are able to generate. Second, businesses cannot simply exploit social issues to generate sales or solve problems. In fact, business value will come from making a sincere commitment to the social issue.

Miracles Don't Happen

Establishing realistic objectives is essential on both the business and social fronts. On the social side, no matter how good, how compelling, how multi-faceted your campaign, it won't bring about instant change. Social change is a long-term, evolutionary process. People don't stop smoking because you tell them they're going to die. They don't give more to a charity simply because it's devoted to a good cause. And they don't reduce energy consumption because someone says they should. Influencing change can only move so far, so fast.

SMB doesn't work business miracles either. You won't double your market share, you won't transform your image, or overcome distribution problems in one fell swoop. Be realistic. Success takes time.

As with any objectives, your social change objectives have to be tied to the marketplace. In this case, it's the Marketplace of Ideas.

Examples of Social Objectives

◆ *Increase awareness/knowledge*

◆ *Change perceptions/attitudes*

◆ *Motivate behaviour change*

◆ *Influence the social climate*

◆ *Influence policy*

◆ *Generate human and financial resources*

◆ *Motivate involvement among private, non-profit, and government sectors*

The Nature of Success

Business success and social success are different. Business success tends to be evaluated against shorter-term measurements than social change, which is a longer-term, evolutionary process (though there are a number of measures that can be used to evaluate SMB program success along the way). The problem occurs when short-term measurements are used to evaluate a long-term process.

A recent study (Drumwright, 1995) illustrates this point. The researcher set out to determine how social campaigns fared relative to product programs. Interestingly, social marketing campaigns were judged more harshly than commercial campaigns. As one respondent put it, the campaign with a social dimension was expected to perform "at least a little better" than a comparable campaign without one. The research points out that "there was a tendency to evaluate social campaigns with longer-term economic and company-oriented objectives with shorter-term measures." So, for example, don't use sales measures to evaluate a campaign designed to enhance relationships with key stakeholders in an effort to influence policy.

The evaluation of a campaign's impact on the social ledger is also often underscored by unrealistic expectations. These expectations generally reflect a lack of understanding of the marketplace of ideas, and of the realities of solving social problems. This leads to disappointment and, often, abandonment of the program if change is not achieved — even if business goals are met.

The Evolution of the Issue

It's important to know how an issue is evolving — where it's been and where it's going. Without the benefit of this understanding, you run the risk of creating programs that don't respond to target group needs. Here's one example.

It is widely assumed that heightened awareness is the solution to the prevention of AIDS. In other words, if people knew more about the disease, then they would adopt healthy lifestyle practices. But research shows that the overwhelming majority of the population knows something about AIDS. Contrary to expectations, awareness has not, by and large, led to health-promoting behaviour.

There is a tendency to think that every social problem can be solved if only people knew more, understood better, thought differently. Not true. Many issues are well known and well understood. But information alone doesn't necessarily lead to behaviour change.

ADD IT UP!

Everything you do communicates and everything you do contributes to the corporate or brand image. Social Marketing for Business is no exception. The SMB program has to reflect and reinforce your image, and it has to add equity to your product or enterprise. That means objectives must be tied to the overall corporate positioning and image goals.

Information alone does not necessarily lead to behaviour change. In the case of AIDS, different intervention strategies are required. Skills development. Role modelling. Creating a culture supportive of safe sex practices. The point is, if you're going to take on the AIDS issue, you need to make the appropriate and necessary contribution to it. A broad awareness campaign might not be what's needed. Your program has to meet a need, not create redundancies. Your objectives for an AIDS program, then, will be influenced by your understanding of the social need. The aspect of the AIDS issue you take on will relate directly to that understanding.

Opinions Count

The success of the program is going to be, in large part, a function of how well it's supported by both internal and external audiences. If your sales force is not on board, for example, you are working with one hand tied behind your back. If key interest groups object to the program, you could generate some backlash. Figure out who matters, and what they think.

Generating and marketing internal and external buy-in is essential to your program. This kind of support is particularly crucial at the outset, when other results may not be immediately forthcoming. The first year of your initiative may be devoted to proving your case as a basis for building momentum in subsequent years.

What to Do

Imagine the Future

Where do you want to be in three to five years in terms of your business, and in terms of your social issue? What are the benefits you would like to reap as a result of an SMB initiative? This kind of visioning exercise is different from establishing short-term, measurable objectives. It is intended to help you think not about the nitty-gritty, but rather the broad business and social change you aim to bring about.

Crunch the Numbers

If your objectives are not based on hard numbers, the program will never really be an integral part of your business strategy. Just as product marketers crunch numbers, social marketers have to be

If your objectives are not based on hard numbers, the program will never really be an integral part of your business strategy.

"It doesn't matter how you get there when you don't know where you're going."

Flying Karamozov Brothers

concerned with hard measurement criteria (this may seem obvious, but it's too often overlooked). If company morale is your problem, for example, determine current levels of absenteeism and productivity. If sales are your problem, look at trends, projections, pricing, competition, distribution, market forces, and so forth. If regulation is your problem, measure the impact of that regulation on your business. If your objective is to increase shelf space, look at how much you're getting and why.

In establishing both business and social objectives, quantify your expectations. Success is relative.

Pick a Priority or Two

Keep focused. Choose one or two areas that you need to improve. Do you want increased sales? Enhanced customer loyalty? Better retailer response?

On the social side, choose a couple of achievable goals. If the environment is your issue, don't take on the whole problem. Instead, you may want to get people to improve the air quality in their homes. If literacy is your issue, you may want to undertake an anti-stigma campaign to change people's perceptions of those who are illiterate. Make sure your objectives are measurable both in the short and the long term.

Establish Baselines

Now that you've determined your program areas, establish clear baselines and realistic objectives. By how much do you want to increase shelf space? How much more traffic do you want through the store in the next three months? Don't forget to establish measurements over time.

Establishing baselines on the social side is more difficult. If your goal is to improve air quality, it's probably better to set baselines for behaviour change. At the start, ascertain how many people are properly storing and disposing of paint products, and how many people are using aerosol cleaners. At the end of the program, measure behaviour change (e.g., 10 per cent less of the sample is using the wrong household products). Don't be discouraged. Any percentage change in the short term is success. Other measures of success include the extent and nature of media coverage, the reaction of stakeholders, and the number of calls you receive about the program (negatives are also important — they tell you where you're going wrong and help you respond in a timely and appropriate manner).

In Review

Defining Success

WHAT TO KNOW

- ❖ **There are two sets of objectives**
  Know how they differ
- ❖ **Miracles don't happen**
  Know what to expect
- ❖ **The nature of success**
  Know its timelines
- ❖ **The evolution of the issue**
  Know where you fit in
- ❖ **Opinions count**
  Know who matters

WHAT TO DO

- ❖ **Imagine the future**
  Look ahead three to five years
- ❖ **Crunch the numbers**
  Be rigorous
- ❖ **Pick a priority or two**
  Be realistic
- ❖ **Establish baselines**
  Define your starting point
- ❖ **Measure success**
  On time, on strategy
- ❖ **Share objectives**
  Market the mission

In establishing both business and social objectives, quantify your expectations. Success is relative. In general, you'll be looking for some kind of change — improve, reduce, prevent or enhance. But compared to what? By how much? In what time frame? Be specific in all areas at the outset, so that you can measure correctly along the way.

Measure Success

There are three important points here. First, build measurements into your program right from the start and make sure they are put on the right timetable. If you evaluate success based on an increase in sales too early, for example, the program will be seen as a failure.

Second, count whatever is relevant to the project. Count savings. Count sales. Count impressions made and decisions taken. Then apply outcomes to the refinement of your program.

Third, make sure you're not comparing apples and oranges. The Drumwright study revealed that where sales objectives were not met, managers tended to ignore competitive factors and to blame the social marketing campaign itself.

Share Objectives

Establishing and promoting program objectives (and short- and long-term successes) can be one of the most powerful tools to motivate your markets. At the outset, you want to rally the troops and generate buy-in by telling audiences what you're about to do. Make sure you talk to the right people, at all levels, both inside and outside the organization. Internally, managers are as vital to the success of the program as senior executives. Externally, the earlier you inform and involve key players, the better your chances of success. Make your presentation to regulators, special interest groups, issue experts, and relevant suppliers.

At key steps along the way, market your results. And at the end, clearly link the program to success in order to lay the groundwork for an evolving program.

Establishing and promoting program objectives (and short- and long-term successes) can be one of the most powerful tools you have to motivate your markets.

TARGETING YOUR AUDIENCES

Hearts and minds rule pocketbooks

Social Marketing for Business, like commercial marketing, stands or falls on an ability to understand and target markets. As with commercial marketing, social marketing is concerned with meeting target group wants and needs. And building relationships around them.

Commercial and social markets are not necessarily one and the same. Consumers of a product and consumers of a program can be different. Molson Breweries' AIDS initiative responds to the concerns of its consumers, but the program primarily works on behalf of people infected with the disease or who fall into risk categories, only a small percentage of whom would also fall into the consumer category.

In some cases, commercial and social markets are exactly the same. For example, the markets for Revlon's *Kiss for the Cure* campaign are the company's consumers as well as the audience for its social marketing program: women.

Even when commercial and issue markets are the same, it's essential to understand the difference between people as consumers and people as social beings. Commercial marketing campaigns appeal to consumer needs and aim to influence consumer behaviour. Social marketing campaigns, on the other hand, must relate to social needs and behaviours in order to be successful. You already have an excellent knowledge of your markets from a commercial point of view. Take a fresh look at these groups in developing your social change programs.

Other business and social audiences must be taken into account as well. Companies must look at the needs and potential roles of traditional publics such as employees, the trade, regulators, shareholders, and so forth. Now you must also take into account the broad range of intermediaries and influencers that are relevant to the market on the social side — gatekeepers, opinion leaders, issue experts and the media.

Success will be a direct result of how insightful you are about the needs and wants of your markets and audiences — as consumers of both products and issues.

Success will be a direct result of how insightful you are about the new set of needs and wants of your markets and audiences — as consumers of both products and issues.

Target Audiences

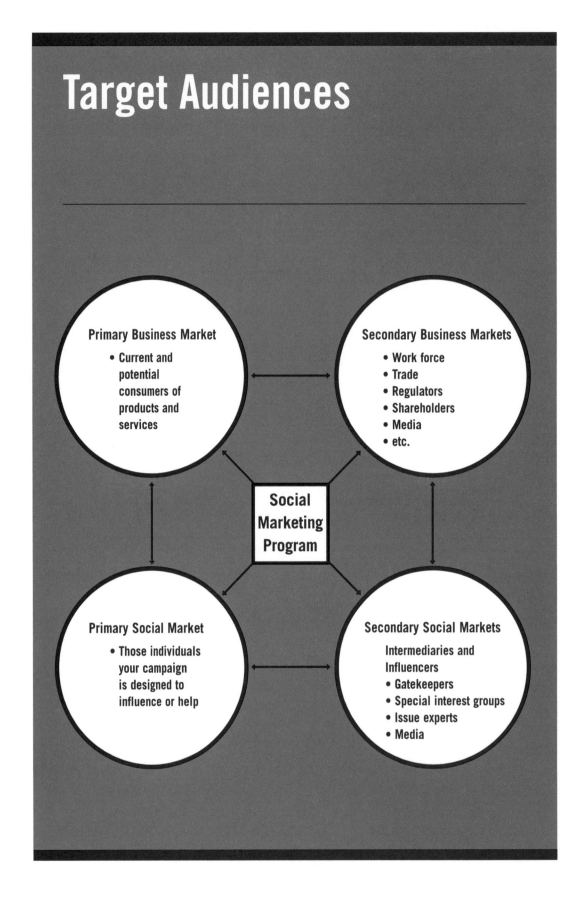

Primary Business Market
- Current and potential consumers of products and services

Secondary Business Markets
- Work force
- Trade
- Regulators
- Shareholders
- Media
- etc.

Social Marketing Program

Primary Social Market
- Those individuals your campaign is designed to influence or help

Secondary Social Markets
Intermediaries and Influencers
- Gatekeepers
- Special interest groups
- Issue experts
- Media

What to Know

Who Your Markets Are

You already have an exceptional knowledge of who your consumers are — demographically, geographically, and psychographically. While this data is integral to developing a profile of your social marketing audience, additional information will be required. You will need to understand the social needs, wants, priorities, perceptions, attitudes, behaviours, values, and beliefs of these groups. This applies to both your consumers and your primary social markets.

It is also imperative that you have an understanding of your secondary business and social markets. Again, you likely have an excellent understanding of your work force, the trade, your suppliers, relevant legislators, and so forth. But now you need to look at them differently, and consider what their attitudes and beliefs are in relation to the social issue with which you have chosen to align yourself. On the social side, you'll need to understand the views, attitudes, needs, and potential roles of influencers and intermediaries.

Where You Stand

It's important to consider how your markets will perceive your social marketing efforts. If you aren't credible, your campaign won't be credible. This is why the decision of program authorship is so important.

The relationship of the government to its markets is one good example. For some audiences, there is little that lends more legitimacy to a program or message than a government logo. In a U.S. campaign to reduce energy consumption, for example, tests found that audiences were far more likely to trust messages put out by the government than by an oil company. But for other markets the opposite is true. In recent focus groups with youth, one government department found that teenagers were more apt to believe the messages of certain corporations, such as Nike or Coca-Cola, than those of the government.

There's a Story Behind the Headlines

When you analyze your markets to determine issue relevance, be careful. There is a tendency to look at top-line results and assume that these findings accurately reflect the attitudes, beliefs, and behaviours of key audiences. Not necessarily. Here's an example. A few years ago,

There is a tendency to look at top-line results and assume that these findings truly represent the attitudes, beliefs and behaviours of key audiences.

Glossary of Terms

☛ **PRIMARY BUSINESS MARKET:** *Current and potential consumers of your products or services.*

☛ **PRIMARY SOCIAL MARKET:** *Those individuals your campaign is designed to influence or help. Also, the group of people whose knowledge, attitudes, beliefs, or behaviour you want to change in order to achieve some social benefit.*

☛ **SECONDARY BUSINESS MARKETS:** *Those audiences connected to your business, who have some stake in its activity and/or success. Secondary business markets can include employees, franchisees, the trade, suppliers, shareholders, the media, etc.*

☛ **SECONDARY SOCIAL MARKETS:** *Consist of intermediaries and influencers.*

☛ **INTERMEDIARIES:** *Those individuals or organizations who stand between you and your primary social target, and have a stake in the outcome of your program. Intermediaries can participate in the development or delivery of your program. They can include program partners, sponsors, gatekeepers, and stakeholders.*

☛ **INFLUENCERS:** *Those people who are in a position to exert direct personal influence over the knowledge, attitudes, beliefs, or behaviour of your primary targets. Influencers include family, peers (friends, co-workers, classmates, colleagues), service providers (teachers, physicians, social workers, etc.), and opinion leaders (celebrities, community leaders, professionals, etc.).*

nationwide surveys exploring concerns on the public's agenda showed that the environment ranked above the economy and job creation. But looking deeper, it turned out that while people were indeed concerned, they were also dispirited, passive, and largely ignorant of the facts. Further, they believed that their small contribution could never really make a difference. If a company chooses to commit itself to the environment, information like this should be the key to program planning. For example, the campaign might focus on personal efficacy. It might present solutions, not problems. It might promote the important progress made by the environmental movement to date, so that people believe results are achievable and effective.

Another example. Focus group after focus group reveals that adolescents believe they would respond to substance abuse advertising that relies on scare tactics, such as "body bag" messages and images. But research measuring behaviour change as a result of these ads shows that, in fact, these advertisements are strong on recall but do not have a substantial impact on behaviour.

No Market is an Island

It's a common mistake to focus on one or two markets only, and forget about the implications of the campaign on others. Cutting out certain groups can fail to maximize potential opportunity and leverage. It can also cause serious problems. A program for consumers, for example, should address the needs of your distributors, packagers, sales force, agents, or franchisees. These groups have to be on board or the program won't work.

Here's one example with an unfortunate result. According to newspaper reports, in the mid-1980s, a then-successful U.S. company, ComputerLand, decided to "see what it could do as a corporation to produce a result that would be both profitable and contribute to the end of world hunger." The company spent a million dollars of its advertising budget to alert corporate America, and to encourage companies to call in for a kit full of ideas on how to get involved. ComputerLand's next step was to link anti-hunger needs with corporate resources.

"Companies that exhibit social consciousness perform better financially when compared to companies that are involved less with social issues."

**Chivas Regal Report
on Working Americans:
Emerging Values for
the 1990s**

What You Need to Know about Your Audiences

Targeting begins with developing a clear and insightful profile of your target markets. To do so, collect and analyze as much information on your audiences as you can. The following provides some lines of inquiry you can pursue to gather the information you need.

You will undoubtedly have much of the data in relation to your consumers, and likely in relation to some of your secondary business markets. But you won't have all of it. These guidelines should help. They will also help you get to know your primary social markets, and look at your consumer markets differently — from a social point of view.

DEMOGRAPHICS: Who are they? What is their age, sex, income, education, ethnicity, language, occupation, family status, literacy level, community size?

GEOGRAPHICS: How is your target population distributed geographically? Are they collected together in a group somehow? Are they broken down into small groups? Do they live in particular kinds of neighbourhoods? Do they work in or travel through particular locations? Are they chiefly urban or rural?

ATTITUDINAL: To what degree are they aware of the problem? How do they perceive it? To what degree do they feel it is personally relevant? Do they feel at risk? How do they explain or justify their current behaviour? Do they feel that the proposed behaviour would make a positive difference to their lives? Do they have the inclination or desire to change? Do they have enough knowledge to recognize the problem? Will they be able to decide to change based on the knowledge they have?

But then the trouble began. The computer industry fell into a slump. Profits declined. ComputerLand franchisees around the world began to blame the hunger program for their business problems. Clearly, the SMB program was not the sole cause of shrinking sales. There were other forces at play. But the program was made the scapegoat because the company's CEO, whose program this was, hadn't bothered to get the buy-in and support of his network.

Conversely, the Canadian Tire Child Protection Foundation works closely with its retailers to promote its program. Dedicated to fostering the health, safety, and welfare of Canadian children through educational programs, the program has in-store displays, police and fire department visits to local retailers, product tie-ins, local events, and board representation by franchisees. The result is a program that works.

Internal Audiences are Key

No matter who you decide to target, it is vital that you include an employee component, or that, at the least, your program is consistent with the values and priorities of your work force. This is not only smart employee relations — there are bottom-line implications as well. According to *The Chivas Regal Report on Working Americans: Emerging Values for the 1990s*, almost half of survey respondents say their loyalty to companies would increase if the corporations were involved in public service activities. Even among those who say their loyalty has decreased in recent years, over one-third (37%) say they would feel more loyal if they knew about the charitable contributions or public service activities of the companies. The report goes on to state that "other research has also found that companies that exhibit social consciousness perform better financially when compared to companies that are involved less with social issues."

Companies that have put these ideas into practice have reaped the rewards. At Tuscon Electronic Power Company, corporate bonding once meant a big dinner at a big hotel with big speeches. Now employees get together to paint buildings, tutor children, and build recreational facilities in inner city areas. According to a company spokesperson, the corporation has not only become more visible in the community, but employees have become more productive because they have company support for something that matters to them personally.

No matter who you decide to target, it is vital that you include an employee component, or that, at the least, your program is consistent with the values and priorities of your work force.

BEHAVIOURAL: If there is risk behaviour, is it chronic or occasional? Under what circumstances does the behaviour occur? Have they tried to change? What barriers (practical, social, psychological) prevent them from changing? Are there feasible behavioural alternatives they could adopt? What are the points at which decisions are made to engage or not to engage in the risk behaviour? Do target groups have the necessary skills to change?

SOCIAL: What are the important social connections (family, co-workers, classmates, etc.)? Are the attitudes, beliefs, or behaviours common within this peer group? Are they encouraged or discouraged, approved or disapproved? Is there social or peer group support for behaviour change?

ACCESS: To what media are the target group exposed? What community services and facilities does the target group use (health, social, recreational, retail, etc.)? To what organizations do they belong (social, religious, professional, etc)? By what sorts of organizations are they employed?

LIFESTYLE: Are there broader lifestyle considerations that are relevant to the current or desired behaviour? Is the target population mainstream or marginalized? Are they risk-takers or risk-avoiders? Do they plan for the future or live for the moment? What are their values, aspirations, and priorities?

The way in which you gather this information will vary. Focus groups, secondary research reviews, expert consultations and surveys may all be appropriate. It depends on what you're looking for, in what detail, and within what time frame.

Source: Achieving Social Change: Insurance Corporation of British Columbia, 1991

Doing good is an important recruitment technique as well. According to Michael Driver, a professor of management at the University of Southern California who tracks the career choices of top business graduates, an increasing number of students at top schools say they want a career that involves a high level of social responsibility. But, he adds, "most companies don't have a clue about how to relate to such notions."

Mainstream Matters

In general, the prudent programs are those that appeal to mainstream audiences. It is important not to become focused on the radical fringe, simply because they are the most outspoken and demand the most attention. This radical fringe does not necessarily represent the concerns and issues of the majority. While you spend your time fighting fires, you may be neglecting a much broader base of current and potential supporters.

Then there are the hard to influence. If you focus your efforts and energies on those who are most difficult to win over, you'll likely waste your time; they're probably never going to change. You can generally eliminate 20 - 25 per cent of your target off the top. These are the people you will never influence. For example, if you're contemplating an anti-smoking campaign, it is not most effective to concentrate resources on hard core smokers. Instead, social marketing theory suggests that efforts should be focused on prevention, and on those individuals and groups more amenable to change.

A middle-of-the-road strategy is usually the wisest. Focus on the segments that are moderately easy to reach and motivate. That's likely where your market, and your consumers are. But don't be misled. Even though the group is mainstream, they are not homogeneous. You'll need to undertake substantial segmentation research to better understand and target them.

Social Marketing Campaigns Rely on Influence

Bringing about social change, in large part, is a function of rallying groups and galvanizing thinking and opinions around key ideas. It is a matter of engaging social dynamics. Changing the perceptions and behaviours of your end target group is often predicated on how well you can influence the influencers — family, friends, teachers, media, gatekeepers, stakeholders, and so forth.

It is important not to become focused on the radical fringe, simply because they are the most outspoken and demand the most attention.

"IT IS MORE IMPORTANT TO KNOW WHAT KIND OF PATIENT HAS THE DISEASE THAN WHAT KIND OF DISEASE HAS THE PATIENT."

Samuel Johnson

What to Do

Once again, research is required. But as previously outlined in "Choosing Your Issues," not all research has to be primary. And you may have already undertaken some of the required research in the context of other sections of this handbook.

Choose Your Targets

Your first task is to identify and prioritize your business and social markets. If you already know what your issue is, the effort will be more defined. On the business side, ask yourself: With whom do you need to establish better relationships? Is there a segment that is consistently fickle or that you want to win back from the competition? Are you attracting the best and the brightest employees? Is employee morale and loyalty a problem? Is impending legislation an issue? Be rigorous in your analysis. The campaign's success will be predicated on its accuracy of focus and its relevance to markets and audiences.

Next, decide if your primary social market is going to be the same as your primary business market (product or service consumers). The Body Shop's *STOP Violence Against Women* social marketing campaign recognized that over 50 per cent of women are abused, which meant that over half its consumer base is experiencing the problem. On the other hand, the company's *Trade Not Aid* program is intended to help communities in the Third World by undertaking fair trading practices. And Levi Strauss's AIDS awareness and prevention program is directed not to consumers, but to employees.

Finally, identify your secondary business and social markets. No matter what type of program you undertake, they will be an important part of it. The best initiatives are multi-faceted and take into account the broader base of audiences. You'll need to think about what role they can play, and how you can best communicate with them.

Analyze Your Markets

There are many lines of inquiry you can pursue to gather the information you require about your various audiences. Identifying your information needs is your first step. Refer to pages 40 and 42 for useful guidelines.

The campaign's success will be predicated on its accuracy of focus and its relevance to markets and audiences.

Audience Analysis: An Overview

	WHAT?	**WHY?**	**WHO?**
Secondary Research	Review and analysis of relevant existing studies, surveys, academic publications, media clippings, trade publications, etc.	Gain knowledge relevant to issues and target groups and ascertain primary research needs	Relevant government departments and agencies, non-profit organizations, etc.
Expert Consultations	Meetings and interviews with those who have expertise relevant to the issues and target groups	Generate input, expertise, information and buy-in to the SMB process	Social scientists, health officials, police, community leaders, academics, etc.
Secondary Business Audience Consultations	One-on-one group meetings with those who have a stake in or will be affected by the SMB program	Generate an understanding of needs, concerns, priorities and challenges, and test SMB program ideas	Trade, sales force, franchisees, regulators, media, shareholders, etc.
Focus Groups	Structured consultations with groups of individuals who share common characteristics	Uncover views, needs, and priorities relevant to proposed SMB program	Current and potential consumers, primary social market
Surveys	Telephone, mail, or in-person	Generate understanding of markets' values, knowledge, attitudes, beliefs, and self-reported behaviours in relation to your social issue	Primary business markets and, if required, primary social markets

Start with a literature review. This includes an assessment of all available studies, surveys, academic publications, media clippings, trade publications and so on. Consult government departments, libraries, universities and other relevant organizations. If your issue is substance abuse, for example, the Addiction Research Foundation in Toronto has a vast array of information on alcohol and other drugs in relation to specific groups. The Canadian Centre for Substance Abuse provides an information clearinghouse service. Health Canada is also a source. Assembling as much secondary research as possible will give you an excellent sense of your social target market needs, and you'll have a clear idea of what primary research you'll need to undertake.

Expert consultations are also an important research tool. Meet with people who have expertise relevant to your issues: social scientists, health officials, police, community leaders, academics, etc. These individuals often have the best understanding of target group needs, either because they have been studying the subject for some time or because they are the front-line workers in closest contact with markets. In some cases, these people will be important secondary social markets, and will serve as intermediaries and/or influencers in your program design. The sooner you understand their role, and the earlier you generate buy-in, the better your chance of success.

You'll also need to consult with your secondary business audiences to gain an understanding of their needs, perspectives and priorities. How do regulators perceive the issues? What about the trade? What role would they be willing to play, if any? Is this a priority issue for them, or would they prefer to participate in another type of program?

It might be a good idea to supplement information gaps by undertaking focus groups, particularly with your consumers. Your consumers will tell you if this issue is right for you, what needs they have, and if a social marketing program would enhance your relationship with customers.

Last, but certainly not least, meet with key departmental heads within your company to ensure that your SMB program is relevant to their needs. It's generally not much use developing a program that doesn't make sense for groups like Human Resources, Marketing, Donations, and Sales. While you don't want to over-consult, the earlier the buy-in, the better your chances of success later.

Reminder

Don't forget to consult with key departmental heads within your company to ensure that your SMB program is relevant to their needs.

In Review

Targeting Your Audiences

WHAT TO KNOW

- **Who your markets are**
  Know them as consumers and
  as people
- **Where you stand**
  Know where you're credible
- **There's a story behind the headlines**
  Dig deep
- **No market is an island**
  Know where you fit in
- **Internal audiences are key**
  Know who matters
- **Mainstream matters**
  Know where to focus your efforts
- **Social marketing campaigns rely on influence**
  Know who influences whom

WHAT TO DO

- **Choose your targets**
  Business, social, and secondary
- **Analyze your markets**
  Do the research
- **Segment your targets**
  By demographics, by social issue
- **Study the competition**
  In all categories

Segment Your Targets

It is widely assumed that certain groups of people think and feel similarly about a social issue, and will respond to programs in a like manner. This simply isn't true. A teenager living with two parents in a higher-income area, and who plans to attend university, has a vastly different outlook on life than his or her counterpart who is truant or living on the streets. Understanding differences is going to affect how you talk to adolescents about drugs, safe sex, and education. It will affect your messages, the language you use, your communication vehicles, and the type of programming you do. It will also affect the kinds of partners you hook up with. So it's vital that you accurately segment your targets.

Segment your consumer market by its relationship to the social issue. Here's an example. Many players in the cosmetics industry have undertaken breast cancer campaigns, largely because the issue is clearly relevant to their primary markets — women. But for the campaigns to be most effective, a company will need to understand who the program markets are. If Cosmetics Company X offers products to consumers ranging from ages 16 to 60, it must understand that the needs of an adolescent versus the needs of an adult versus the needs of a senior are different not only in product consumption, but also in relation to breast cancer information and programming. This, in turn, will affect how Company X conceives its initiative, establishes its positioning and messages, and undertakes its promotion.

Study the Competition

Determine who else has a social agenda targeting your business and social markets. Don't limit yourself to your industry or category competitors. It's essential that McDonald's knows and understands Imperial Oil's program aimed at kids. And don't limit yourself to your sector. Find out which governments and non-profits are targeting your groups. Find out what's being done, and what the results have been to date. Your findings will tell you whether entry into this arena is appropriate for you. They'll tell you how to approach the issue and your market for maximum differentiation.

Targeting your audience provides the basis for all subsequent planning decisions: choosing your partners, developing your positioning, and creating your programming and promotional activities.

It is widely assumed that certain groups of people think and feel similarly about a social issue, and will respond to programs in a like manner. This simply isn't true.

ESTABLISHING PARTNERSHIPS

One plus one equals three

Corporations commonly develop their social marketing programs in partnership with non-profit organizations or government bodies. The process can be challenging. Generally, the private sector company, the non-profit group, and the government organization operate with different mandates, agendas, priorities, and processes. Don't be discouraged, however. Given the right fit, and the right relationship, there may be no more powerful or effective SMB mechanism.

Why bother establishing partnerships in the first place? There are two compelling reasons: credibility and social benefit. The right non-profit, or the right government body, can lend a corporation the credibility it could never garner on its own. Corporations are not issue experts. They are not, first and foremost, in the business of social change. Most non-profit and public sector organizations are. Becel Margarine is committed to promoting a heart healthy diet and has built its marketing strategy around that. What makes the commitment all the more credible and compelling is its public education program, undertaken in collaboration with the Heart and Stroke Foundation.

In terms of social benefit, it is becoming increasingly clear that no single organization can bring about widespread social change on its own. Times have changed. Today, the problems are more complex, the issues more pervasive. Non-profits are still reeling from the effects of a long and hard recession. Governments can no longer afford to be the primary agents of change they once were. In most instances, what's required is a collaborative, collective effort for social change that extends far beyond the capabilities of one or two organizations.

There is an additional reason for getting involved in partnerships that shouldn't be overlooked: there is sometimes no choice. The non-profit world often tends to look unkindly upon corporations that are encroaching on their territory, or that are undertaking initiatives inconsistent with perceived priorities and needs. Again, the Avon saga is pertinent. According to reports, it seems that while the company made a sincere commitment to supporting the fight against breast cancer, it did not work with the more established breast cancer organizations. The company was vilified by issue

Partnerships allow for a collaborative, collective effort for social change that extends far beyond the capabilities of one or two organizations.

"There must be a

division not only

of profits, but a

division also of

responsibilities."

Louis D. Brandeis

groups. Avon persevered, however, and the result is an extremely successful and important cause-related marketing program. But the politics don't appear to have been easy.

Partnerships are generally struck in one of two ways. Most often, non-profit organizations or governments approach corporations with a sponsorship program. Less frequently, the corporation creates its own social marketing program and searches out the non-profit or government department that offers the best fit. Either way, the corporation must act according to its own agenda, objectives, and priorities.

It is vital that corporations do the up-front work if they are going to make sound, informed decisions about their social change agendas. A corporate social change agenda requires the same rigorous thinking and planning that is applied to product marketing. Even if you opt to wait for organizations to approach you with partnership opportunities, make sure you go through the exercise of determining who you want to reach, for what purpose, for how long, and with what issue focus. Organized, far-sighted planning will prevent the piecemeal approach that is characteristic of too many corporate campaigns.

In 1992, the federal government announced a 10 per cent cut in grants and subsidies to various government-supported programs, translating into about $1.8 billion by 1995.

Maclean's

What to Know

The more you deal with up front, the better your chances for a successful relationship. Get to know each other. Here are some guidelines you can follow to help ensure a productive relationship.

Compatibility is Vital

Make sure the partner you choose has a philosophy and ideology similar to your own. You don't want to get involved with organizations that are radical (unless, of course, you're a radical company). For example, while some animal rights groups may provide a warm and comforting image for you, those who equate the value of a rat's life with that of a human's might not leave you with the type of profile you're after.

Criteria for Partnership

✔ *Common target groups*

✔ *Appropriate mandate*

✔ *Compatible image*

✔ *Geographic fit (e.g., national, regional, local)*

✔ *Influential with consumers*

✔ *Well-respected*

✔ *Sound financial practices*

✔ *Adequate opportunity for profile*

✔ *Value-added leverage*

✔ *Opportunities for product tie-ins and promotion*

✔ *History of good relations*

✔ *Acceptable timetable*

Accountability Counts

Most non-profits are as good as their word. Nevertheless, it is important that you go into any partnership with an assurance that the organization is managed prudently and judiciously, and that the most money possible is going to the issues and the people the non-profit is mandated to help. Don't hesitate to ask for detailed accounts of operations and allocation of funds.

Corporations should also be clear about the nature and substance of the partnership. Program details should be discussed up front, including issues relating to roles and responsibilities, deliverables and outcomes. Whether you are partnering with a non-profit or government organization, make sure that all the details are worked out well in advance, and that they are documented and shared with both sides.

Whether you are partnering with a non-profit or government organization, make sure that all the details are worked out well in advance, and that they are documented and shared with both sides.

Mutual Benefit is Key

The days of corporate giving with no return appear to be pretty well gone. Corporations are looking for win-win opportunities. For many, a listing or small logo on the back of an educational brochure is no longer sufficient. Consider what the non-profit has to offer you. Do you share a similar target market? Can you access the non-profit's distribution system? Will you be able to reach new markets? Are there opportunities for product tie-ins or product promotions? Can the organization offer you issue or market intelligence? Will the non-profit share its database with you? Will you have consumer category exclusivity? It is important to get these issues on the table prior to agreeing to a partnership.

Expectations Must be Shared

Non-profit organizations, government agencies and corporations have mandates, agendas and priorities that are fundamentally different. Corporations are driven to produce profits, non-profits to address social agendas, and governments to create policies. Corporations work on fairly tight planning cycles; the decision-making process of both non-profits and government can be long and involve many people. This does not mean you cannot have productive and mutually beneficial relationships. It does mean, however, that everything has to be spelled out from the start.

Two of the areas of greatest friction are program ownership and identity. Recently, a major brand went into partnership with a professional association. The brand had given the promised amount

Partnership Guidelines: A Checklist

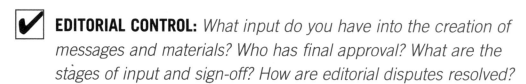 **EDITORIAL CONTROL:** *What input do you have into the creation of messages and materials? Who has final approval? What are the stages of input and sign-off? How are editorial disputes resolved?*

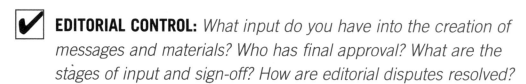 **CORPORATE/BRAND IDENTIFICATION:** *Is the program jointly authored by you and your partner? What type of identity will you have? What size will your logo be? Where will it be located? Are there opportunities for corporate messages? Where do they appear? How many can there be? Will you have partner identification on any of your own materials?*

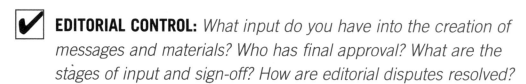 **PARTNER IDENTIFICATION:** *What type of identity will your partner have? What size will its logo be? Where will it be located? Are there opportunities for corporate messages? What are they? Where do they appear? How many can there be?*

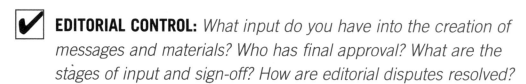 **CORPORATE/BRAND ENDORSEMENT:** *What are the opportunities to have your partner endorse your products or services? What are the parameters — time, money, approvals, etc.?*

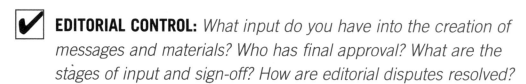 **OWNERSHIP:** *Who holds the program copyright? Who owns the materials? What are the production or collateral use rights? What are the territories covered (Canada, U.S., international)?*

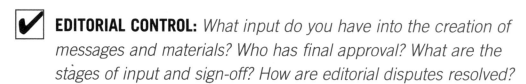 **DISTRIBUTION:** *Whose responsibility is it? What are the costs? Timelines?*

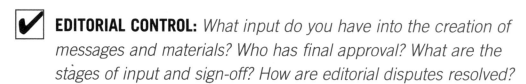 **PROMOTION:** *Who's doing what? Who's paying for what? Are there opportunities for spin-off promotions? Will your senior executives or celebrity spokespersons be available for promotional purposes?*

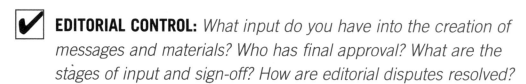 **MONEY:** *Who's paying for what? Will there be revenue? If so, how will it be utilized (self-liquidation, investment in future programs, donation funds, etc.)?*

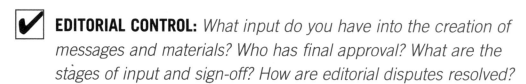 **TERM:** *What is the length of the partnership agreement? Are there options for program renewal? What is the timeline for program planning?*

of money, and just as the program was going to press, brand managers noticed that their logo did not appear on the material. When they insisted their brand get recognition, the association balked, claiming that they didn't feel comfortable with that kind of message and image. Needless to say, the brand was horrified, having just committed a substantial amount of money to the program, only to receive nothing in return. These are details that must be worked out in advance. Decide on execution — who's going to do what? Decide on the approvals process. Decide on promotion — who's doing media relations? Decide on distribution — who is responsible for making sure the program reaches its markets?

What to Do

Establish Guidelines
Your first task is to set out your policies and procedures for working with non-profits and government. Be as comprehensive as possible. Define what you're looking for in a non-profit, and what it will take to get you involved. Create a checklist for evaluation.

Do Your Homework
Find out everything there is to know about the organization in question. What is its mandate? Its policies? Its politics? What does the organization believe in? How does it work? How much of its money goes to the cause, and how much to administration? Has the group ever partnered before? If so, what was the nature of these partnerships? Were they successful? How is the organization perceived by key markets? Where does it stand on issues? Who are its supporters? Detractors? What kind of social change results can the organization demonstrate?

Conducting the background check should include reviewing organizational documents such as annual reports, strategies, promotional materials, balance sheets, and any available studies. It should include a comprehensive media search. You can also ask for references.

Your non-profit partners are not your suppliers. That means they work with you, not for you. Many partnerships have failed because corporations assume that non-profits should be grateful for what they're getting. This kind of thinking is a recipe for disaster.

In Review

Establishing Partnership

WHAT TO KNOW

- **Compatibility is vital**
  Know your ideology, know theirs
- **Accountability counts**
  Know your partner's history
- **Mutual benefit is key**
  Know your opportunities
- **Expectations must be shared**
  Know where you fit in

WHAT TO DO

- **Establish guidelines**
  Set out your policies and procedures
- **Do your homework**
  Check out your partner
- **Consult**
  Jointly determine the program and relationship parameters
- **Contract**
  Get it down on paper
- **Collaborate**
  Manage the relationship

Consult

Once you have a sense of who this organization is, sit down with its representatives. Get all the issues on the table. Tell them what you want, how you work, what you expect from the relationship, and what you're willing to give them. For example, you'll likely want category exclusivity. You'll want your logo a certain size. You probably want spin-off and media opportunities. You may want product tie-ins or distribution.

Make sure there is a concrete understanding of non-profit versus business needs and demands. Jointly develop the program's mission statement, and ascertain what it means for each group. Determine how long you'll work together. Is this a one-shot deal? Or will you be embarking on a long-term relationship that may include numerous projects?

Most important, figure out how you're going to work together. What are the roles and responsibilities of each party? How do you make decisions? How do they? How long do approvals take? With whom would you be working? Does this include staff and volunteers? It's important to establish a shared vision and protocol for the relationship right from the start and to get them down on paper for later reference.

Contract

Don't leave your relationship to a verbal agreement. Everyone remembers things just a little differently. Create a simple, clear contract that sets out what the program or partnership is, who's responsible for what, timelines, money, rights and obligations, expectations, and options for a longer-term relationship.

Collaborate

Once the deal has been struck, don't disappear. The relationship is just beginning. Establish the liaison and the mechanisms required to build and manage a successful relationship. Figure out how you're going to work together through the three stages of the program: development, implementation, and evaluation. Remember, establishing partnerships isn't the same as maintaining them.

Make sure there is a concrete understanding of non-profit versus business needs and demands. Jointly develop the program's mission statement, and ascertain what it means for each group.

POSITIONING THE ISSUE

Brand It!

The importance of positioning springs from the premise that perception is reality. How markets see an issue, how relevant the issue is, and how willing they are to act are all essential elements of the social marketing challenge.

You have to capture attention in a very busy marketplace. But that's just the start. In order to gain influence, you'll have to establish a relationship of trust and authority. And then you have to deliver on the expectations you've created by providing programs that meet market needs and satisfy wants.

None of this is new. Companies apply this kind of thinking to their everyday business and marketing activity. Now you must do so in the social marketing arena, where the process tends to be a little more abstract. The generic social idea has to be transformed into a distinctly branded product that generates buy-in, motivates action, and accrues benefit to its source — your brand or business.

The positioning framework — and the brand and message strategies based on it — are central to your ability to build program equity. In other words, before you begin to develop your program, you need the Big Idea. Everything hinges on it.

The generic social idea has to be transformed into a distinctly branded product that generates buy-in, motivates action, and accrues benefit to its source — your brand or business.

What to Know

Issues Start Off Generic

Laundry detergent is generic. So are financial services. Differentiating these products is a matter of creating and articulating their unique characteristics and then communicating them to markets in the most compelling manner possible. Social issues are no different. Violence, substance abuse, diseases, women's rights, international development — all are generic issues. How you define an issue, and the orientation you take to it, will differentiate both the issue and the product or company attached to it.

Nothing is as Powerful as an Idea Whose Time Has Come

An old cliché, but true. From a social marketing perspective, the challenge is to harness the power of ideas by positioning and packaging them for maximum relevance and impact.

Positioning Statement
A Checklist

You need two positioning platforms or statements: one for the issue and one for the author of the program — your company or brand.

ISSUE POSITIONING

☑ *Is your positioning statement clear, compelling, and long term?*

☑ *Is your take on the issue distinctive in comparison to others?*

☑ *Does it stake out the issue territory you need to occupy?*

☑ *Is it compatible with the missions and mandates of your potential partners?*

☑ *Does it have a projected lifespan of at least three years?*

CORPORATE/BRAND POSITIONING

☑ *What is your role in relation to the program? Does your corporation serve as catalyst, information or service broker, promoter, etc.?*

☑ *Is there image consistency between your company or brand and the issue and program?*

This is easier said than done. Most ideas are old, and many of them are tired. They've lost impact. They have to be re-thought, re-formed, and revitalized. The most prominent example is fitness. From a marginalized activity that, in the early 1970s, was practised only by kids, health nuts, and athletes, to a mainstream obsession a decade later, to a declining pursuit today, fitness has come full circle. In order to re-capture the imagination of markets in relation to issues, you need to understand how the issues are perceived now, and how they should be framed and positioned later.

Most ideas are old, and many of them are tired. They've lost impact. They have to be re-thought, re-formed, and revitalized.

Issues Generate Concern but Ideas Drive Action

Issues or causes that are shared and promoted often generate response — usually in the form of money thrown at the problem. But that's no longer enough. There are too many causes. Too many appeals. Too many organizations in desperate need of time and money. The result is donor fatigue.

People are increasingly looking for the idea that leads to a solution. They are looking for action they can take to make a difference. Everyone's got problems. Who's got answers?

Nike's *PLAY* program does. The issue is youth alienation and the threat it poses to society. The audience is every one of us. The source, of course, is the largest and most influential maker of sports apparel in the world. The message is a positive one, and the action track is viable. The positioning platform is: "Imagine the world without sports". The images are of social unrest: inner city children who, denied the chance to play basketball, join street gangs instead. People are motivated by evocative messages to call a 1-800 number and "Participate in the Lives of American Youth" (the program has recently come to Canada as "Participate in the Lives of All Youth"). On the ground, Nike has engineered a community action program that gives volunteers things to do and ways to participate. Nike is succeeding in galvanizing social involvement around an issue that otherwise might have fallen into the abyss of social needs and problems. The company is creating a powerful and unassailable niche for itself, by positioning the issue in terms of its own business — sports.

12 Kinds of Message Strategies

1. **FEAR:** *Many health promotion campaigns use fear or scare tactics in an effort to change behaviour. While these kinds of appeals can be effective in some cases, a great deal of research has shown that if there is too much fear, audiences will ignore the message.*

2. **CONSISTENCY:** *After committing themselves to a position, even in a cursory way, people are more likely to behave in a manner consistent with that position. That's why many programs try to get people to wear buttons or use bumper stickers in support of their cause.*

3. **AUTHORITY:** *People are more willing to follow the suggestions of someone they perceive to be an authority in terms of knowledge or trustworthiness. This is why it is often critical for corporations to align themselves with a non-profit organization that has issue expertise.*

4. **SOCIAL VALIDATION:** *People are more likely to act or subscribe to a belief when they see that others are doing so. This kind of appeal is also called the "bandwagon effect." Social marketing makes as much or more use of this message strategy as commercial marketing, largely because social change is a function of establishing new social norms.*

5. **GUILT:** *While many campaigns rely on guilt to grab attention and solicit support, the trend is shifting to more positive, inspiring messages because of the recognition that guilt messages tend to foster feelings of apathy, frustration, and helplessness.*

6. **MORAL MESSAGES:** *These appeals are directed to the audience's sense of what is right and proper. They are often used to exhort people to support such social causes as a cleaner environment, better race relations, equal rights, and aiding the disadvantaged.*

Source Positioning Is Priority #1

According to *Market Vision 2000*, product and service quality and cost are no longer the sole determining purchase factors. Source credibility is a key variable. The better you are able to link your social agenda to the identity and image of your brand or company, the more leverage your conventional marketing efforts will have. In other words, you need to gain the confidence and trust of your markets in order for them to listen to your messages.

PLAY is exemplary because there is credibility on two fronts. The company is the acknowledged leader in sports, and is endorsed by such celebrity superstars as Michael Jordan and Jackie Joyner-Kersee (in Canada, Silken Laumann). On the community and issue front, the program is credible in large part because Nike's non-profit partner is the Boys and Girls Clubs of America, a well-respected grass roots organization.

Source credibility is a function of perceived commitment. You must demonstrate that you're serious, and that you're in it for the long haul. Companies should not use SMB programs like they would a contest, price discount, or other short-term, sales-focused marketing activities. Your marketplace will not take you seriously if you fail to commit over time.

But credibility is not the only essential issue when considering your source positioning. You also need to define your role in relation to your initiative. For example, The Prudential Insurance Company of America, Canadian Operations, is committed to supporting community action and development. The company positions itself as a *catalyst* to the social change process. Its role is to lead and model behaviour for other private sector companies in an effort to promote involvement and raise the issue on the public agenda. There are other ways for companies to position themselves in relation to their issues. Tele-Direct is taking a *brokering* role — the company uses its Yellow Pages to link target groups with organizations that are dedicated to helping those with literacy needs. Imperial Oil is positioning itself as an *agenda-setter*. It is establishing its corporate leadership by helping ensure the well-being of Canadian kids who are currently "at-risk" or disadvantaged.

Nike is succeeding in galvanizing social involvement around an issue that otherwise might have fallen into the abyss of social needs and problems.

7. **PEER INFLUENCE:** *Often, target groups are most easily influenced by members of their own age, race, cultural or socio-economic background because they can identify with them.*

8. **TESTIMONIAL:** *These messages are based on the assumption that audiences will respond to those who have tried and like the product being tested. Imperial Oil's KAPOW television advertising features a student who has benefited significantly from the program talking about his experience.*

9. **HUMOUR:** *Positive emotional appeals, such as humour, love, pride, and joy are often used by communicators. The upbeat, friendly, and humorous tone used in the ParticipACTION campaign was instrumental in establishing fitness as a desirable and fun activity that everyone could enjoy. Humour can be dangerous, however, particularly around social issues. It should be used only with the greatest care.*

10. **BENEFITS:** *Some messages are designed to appeal to rational thought and decision-making. These messages present information that serves the audience's self-interest.*

11. **CELEBRITY:** *Using celebrities to promote ideas and product is based on the notion that target groups identify with certain public personalities and will therefore want to adopt the behaviours these celebrities endorse. Candice Bergen is the spokesperson for Sprint, the long-distance service. Kurt Browning endorses Coke. And a host of NBA stars promote the Stay in School program.*

12. **RECIPROCITY:** *People often comply with another's request because they feel they owe that person something, often when they would have otherwise declined and even when what they agree to do is more than what they received earlier. That's why some non-profit organizations, for example, hand out flowers or buttons for free.*

Source: Achieving Social Change: Insurance Corporation of British Columbia, 1991

Stake Out Your Territory

The territorial imperative tells you to find your piece of ground, stake it out, and set up social marketing camp there. In other words, own your niche. For example, youth is an enormously popular issue. Yet look at how many companies have taken on youth-related issues without trampling on each other's territory. McDonald's has defined itself in relation to families of sick kids. Canadian Tire is committed to kids and safety. Imperial Oil invests in "at-risk" and disadvantaged kids. YTV addresses youth and achievement.

AIDS is another issue that has inspired significant corporate commitment, yet different companies have managed to attach themselves to different aspects of the issue. Molson Breweries is known for supporting AIDS-related cultural charities. Levi Strauss is renowned for its long-standing commitment to promoting prevention and education of AIDS to its employees and their families. M·A·C Cosmetics has undertaken a cause-related marketing program in support of AIDS research and prevention.

The territorial imperative tells you to find your piece of ground, stake it out, and set up social marketing camp there. In other words, own your niche.

What to Do

Study History

Study the issue. Find out where it's come from, and determine where it's going. This point was addressed in Chapter I, "Choosing Your Issues", but it's worth reiterating here. The only way to truly understand where market opportunity exists is to understand the prevalence and relevance of the issue to its various markets over time. Consider fitness. If you glance at the fitness landscape, you'll likely see that the most opportune area for issue positioning is with people over the age of 40. They've been indoctrinated with the fitness message. They buy it. But now their bodies have changed. What worked for them at 30 is no longer effective. They want to get fit; they just don't have the tools or the know-how. Every issue has a window like this one; the challenge is to find it.

Look Ahead

What is the issue going to look like three years down the road? Five years? And in the next decade? Issues change, as do people's relationships to them. If you're attached to an out-dated issue, you look out of sync with your markets. Or you may find that the issue is gaining

In Review

Positioning the Issue

WHAT TO KNOW

- **Issues start off generic**
  Know your platform
- **Nothing is as powerful as an idea whose time has come**
  Know where your opportunities lie
- **Issues generate concern but ideas drive action**
  Know the power of solutions
- **Source positioning is priority #1**
  Know where you're credible
- **Stake out your territory**
  Know your place

WHAT TO DO

- **Study history**
  Chart the issue's life cycle
- **Look ahead**
  Find out where the issue is going
- **Choose the angle**
  Establish your position
- **Brand it!**
  Package and promote
- **Test**
  Before you go out the door

currency — but with markets to which you are not connected. The idea is not to simply attach yourself to the issue that's most popular, or trendy — the "cause-of-the-week." Rather, your goal is to attach yourself to the issue that is most relevant to your business and your markets, and to which you can make a long-term commitment.

Choose the Angle

Ask yourself the hard questions. What relates best to your company? To your markets? To your current positioning platform? As part of its commitment to being "the responsible car company," Nissan Canada is taking a leadership role in the area of seniors. The company is galvanizing Canadians of all ages to acknowledge and celebrate the contribution seniors have made and continue to make to our country.

Brand It!

Don't leave your positioning up in the air. What's required is the conceptual, strategic, and creative packaging of your ideas. As with corporate and product marketing, this includes considerations of message, identity, tone, and image.

Articulate positioning platforms for both the issue and your corporation. Within the context of these platforms, develop your message strategies. You have some major decisions to make here. For example, do you want to position your issue in terms of its problem or its solution? Do you want your audiences to relate to the risks (e.g., "if you smoke, you'll die"), or to the benefits of the new behaviour (e.g., "giving up smoking is socially appealing")? If the issue is substance abuse and the target is women, will you focus on reducing use by communicating the harmful effects of alcohol or drugs? Or will you take a broader approach to the issue by talking about root causes — like stress and the need for more effective coping mechanisms? What about your company? What messages need to be promoted concerning your role and positioning? Will you be in the business of substance abuse or women and health?

Test

Once you've got your positioning platforms and message strategies, test them. Conduct focus groups. As with product development and commercial campaigns, you need to know how markets will respond. Too many campaigns have gone out the door without the right testing, only to offend or miss the mark.

Don't leave your positioning up in the air. What's required is the conceptual, strategic, and creative packaging of your ideas.

DEVELOPING YOUR PROGRAM

Make change, not noise

Y ou've chosen your issue, selected your markets, set your objectives, decided on your partners, and positioned your issue. The measure of your social marketing insight and skill is predicated on its execution — the program you create.

Programming is the process by which you organize, package, and promote your ideas and resources. It is a matter of translating the knowledge you've gained and the decisions you've made into action.

There is no one program formula that will fix a given problem. However, there are guidelines and options. Most important, there are critical, strategic decisions that you will need to make at every stage of the programming process.

What to Know

How People Change
Social marketing is based on attitude and behaviour change theory, including models of behaviour modification, cognitive and decision-making theories, motivation, risk communication, and learning theory. The social marketer must have at the least a working knowledge of these theories (see pages 72 and 74). Programs risk failure when marketers apply a commercial understanding of consumers to the process of changing social attitudes and behaviours.

The Six Ps of the Social Marketing Mix
Where product marketing has four Ps, social marketing has six — Product, Place, Price, Promotion, People and Policy.

Product
Deciding on your program elements is probably the most difficult step (see pages 76 and 78 for program options). Each has its own merits and drawbacks. Part of your decision will be a function of the kind of campaign you're developing. For example, if you're embarking on an awareness and attitude program to affect the social climate, you'll likely do an advertising campaign, because it provides you with high profile and broad reach. A good example is Labatt's *Know When to Draw the Line* campaign, a highly visible mass-media program that creates a climate supportive of responsible drinking. If you're looking at a skills-based behaviour change campaign, on the

Programming is the process by which you organize, package, and promote your ideas and resources. It is a matter of translating the knowledge you've gained and the decisions you've made into action.

Social Needs and Programming Strategies

Why don't people quit smoking when they find out it can kill them? Why don't we all wear seat belts? Give to charity? Practice safe sex? Become literate? Care for the environment? There are theories to explain the reasons why. These theories are the underpinning of effective social marketing.

The family of theories most relevant to the individual and collective change process are:
- *theories about what people think and believe*
- *theories about how people learn*
- *theories about what people feel*
- *theories about interpersonal relationships*
- *theories about mass communication and persuasion*

While space limitation makes it impossible to cover all the literature, the following outlines some social theories, as well as the type of social marketing interventions that are commonly used in strategy, programming, and message development.

EXAMPLES OF SOCIAL NEEDS

DENIAL: *One of the most common defense mechanisms, the "It won't happen to me" syndrome, is particularly prevalent among people who experiment with cigarettes or drugs, drink and drive, or practice unsafe sex.*

LEARNED HELPLESSNESS: *The expectation that self-protective behaviours will not be successful, and that outcomes are uncontrollable.* **Universal helplessness** *is much the same, and suggests that an outcome is independent of one's own actions as well as the behaviour of others. This is why campaigns that rely too heavily on portraying problems (e.g., international development, the environment) lose their effectiveness over time.*

FEAR: *While fear-arousing communications do indeed generate fear among target audiences, the result is not always the desired behaviour. According to studies, fear can cause anger and make people feel that the message is manipulative. It can also leave people feeling fatalistic. As a result, they resign themselves to the danger. In fact, literature suggests that if people are predisposed to responding in a particular way when in a fearful state, and if no concrete guidance is given, a fear-arousing message only confirms and strengthens existing attitudes and behaviours.*

other hand, you'll probably need to consider information programming (booklets, pamphlets, brochures, videos, etc.) and skills development (workshops, seminars, one-on-one instruction, etc.). The Pharmaceutical Manufacturers Association of Canada launched a program called *Knowledge Is the Best Medicine* to help seniors better manage their medication use. The program consists of brochures on how to use medication properly, a television ad, a 1-800 line for both the profession and the public, and a workshop video and guide for delivery by seniors' organizations in communities across the country.

Advocacy or issue leadership is yet another program type. Here, your audiences will likely be opinion leaders, gatekeepers, policy makers, and the media. Appropriate vehicles for these groups might include issue reports, think pieces, editorials, and speeches. It is unlikely, of course, that any single product will be sufficient. Your program will probably be the orchestration of a variety of elements.

Place

If your social product doesn't get into the hands of your markets, you won't reach their hearts and minds. Too often, programs are left on the shelf because distribution has not been factored in from the start. Then the program is seen as a failure. Years ago, ParticipACTION created a booklet on fitness to be distributed through a major supermarket chain. The program failed, not because of its quality, but because the booklets never made it beyond the stock room — they simply weren't displayed.

On the other hand, ParticipACTION's *Fitness: The Facts* was one of its most successful programs, in large part because it used available delivery channels to best advantage. The program was designed in response to corporations' desire to promote physical fitness in the workplace, without the burdensome costs of building facilities or subsidizing memberships in a health club. *Fitness: The Facts* was a self-assessment and motivational kit that helped people get fit on their own. It was invaluable for overcoming a logistical problem that would have impeded corporate participation in staff health and well-being. The key? The program could be delivered by the mail room. During its first year, over 250,000 employees received materials. Evaluation studies indicated that the program was extremely well-received. It enhanced employee relations, increased fitness knowledge and motivated fitness activity.

Programming Tip #1: A Project Is Not a Program

If you're getting into the business of social change, you can't think short term. This is a long-term initiative. Social benefit does not come about overnight, nor does bottom-line benefit to your corporation. Think in terms of at least three years.

SELF-EFFICACY: *An individual's perception that he or she is either capable, or incapable of performing a certain behaviour. People often doubt their self-efficacy in part because of unfamiliar situations, past failures, or self-protective behaviours. For example, research shows that immigrant or minority women are less likely to access legal services, even when required, largely for fear that they don't have the skills (e.g., language, culture, education) to be effective consumers of the system. Useful interventions often include skills development and role modelling.*

SELECTED SOCIAL CHANGE INTERVENTIONS

DIFFUSION OF INNOVATION: *The process by which an idea, technology, or product is introduced, spread, and then adopted by a target group. Broadly, there are different categories of "adopters," ranging from early to late. Both commercial and social marketers usually attempt to identify early adopters so that they can be targeted first, assuming that the campaign will gain momentum over time and will build enough critical mass to address the harder-to-reach groups later on.*

OBSERVATIONAL LEARNING: *A social learning theory tool, observational learning is a person's tendency to learn behaviour by watching others. Role modelling is a key element, and usually comes in the form of testimonials from celebrities, opinion leaders, or respected peers or colleagues.*

PEER INFLUENCE: *A peer influencer campaign targets those individuals within specific groups who can influence the perceptions, attitudes, and behaviours of their peers. Once these individuals have adopted the desired behaviour, they become models for the rest of the group. Peer-assisted learning programs such as* Weight Watchers *fall into this category.*

DECISION THEORIES: *In general, these theories hold that people act rationally and will make choices that will help them avoid negative experiences. For some people, this is true. When the Surgeon General announced in 1963 that smoking is harmful to our health, a significant number of smokers quit immediately. The presentation of clear, accurate, and compelling information delivered through a credible source can be the most effective intervention with these audiences.*

Think about your program within the context of available delivery channels. Most corporations have a range of vehicles such as media, retail outlets, sales forces, and franchisees, as well as the distribution channels of their non-profit partner. Understand the power and leverage of each, and capitalize on what you have at your disposal. For example, if you have access to physicians' offices, then consider creating products that can be accessed through that channel. Similarly, if you have retail stores as part of your distribution system, your campaign might be built around a point-of-purchase program.

Price

Social products — such as seminars, courses, kits and resource manuals — can either be delivered for a cost, or for free. The downside to charging a fee is that it limits access to the program. But the advantage is that your program will attract those individuals who truly want to make change. Further, research shows that people who pay for products or services are more likely to value them. In the end, you'll get a crowd that's committed and that will take your program seriously.

There is another problem that can arise if your program is free of charge. If it's successful, it can break the bank. Here's an example. Years ago, Colgate and the Canadian Dental Association (CDA) partnered to produce *First Teeth*, a program to help parents better care for their children's dental health. The program consisted of a booklet for parents on how to care for their children's teeth, a wall chart for kids, and posters for display in the dental office. Initially, the kit was distributed through the dental office at no charge.

Demand was overwhelming. Over 80 per cent of the profession ordered the program. Colgate had a problem. It could not afford to continue to produce it for free. Together, Colgate and the CDA decided that the program should be sold to dentists. Demand dropped to manageable rates. And because *First Teeth* became self-financing, it is still in existence today. It is considered one of Colgate's and the CDA's most successful initiatives.

The objective of your pricing strategy, of course, is not to generate revenue (unless it's a fund-raising tool for a non-profit), but to develop a self-financing social product that can be offered over the long term.

Programming Tip #2:

A Keychain Is Not

a Campaign

Single tactics won't work. Don't think brochure, or poster, or wallet card. You've got to think about the full programming arsenal you have at your disposal. The only way to bring about change, the only way to get your program seen, is to create a multi-faceted campaign that relies upon the mutually reinforcing effects of multiple programming lines.

Social Marketing at Work: Tools for Change

Social marketing employs many of the tools and media generally used to promote products and services. Here is a rundown of these programming options.

ADVERTISING
- Provides high profile, high awareness, broad reach
- Raises an issue on the social agenda, builds motivation, provides behavioural models, creates social momentum
- Does not allow for detailed information delivery or skills development

MEDIA PROGRAMMING
- Includes TV specials, radio features, magazine supplements, and other mass media
- Provides in-depth coverage and detailed information
- Allows for product re-packaging and distribution through alternative channels

MEDIA RELATIONS
- SMB initiatives generally provide excellent material for the media, and most programs have been covered extensively

INFORMATION PROGRAMMING
- Includes booklets, pamphlets, brochures, filmstrips, videos, on-line, etc.
- Should contain not just information, but practical and motivating advice

TRAINING/SKILLS DEVELOPMENT
- Includes counselling, workshops, classroom, self-help, and one-on-one instruction
- Generally reaches only a limited audience
- To increase reach and distribution, programmers can institute a "train-the-trainer" model

ADVOCACY/ISSUE LEADERSHIP
- Includes special reports ("think pieces" or research reports), editorials, newsletters, presentations, speeches, meetings, conferences, or symposia
- Used to move your issue up on the public agenda, particularly with opinion leaders, gatekeepers, policy makers, etc; can also be used to build coalitions

Promotion

Some corporations question the ethics of promoting their good works. Conventional thinking has been that it's wrong to capitalize on what should be an altruistic act. In fact, the exact opposite is true.

If this is an ethical concern for you, then look at it this way. Social change is largely a function of creating social momentum, of galvanizing support and commitment from a broad-based constituency. How can this be achieved if your efforts are not promoted? Addressing social issues can no longer be confined to those organizations that lack the ways and the means of raising the issues on the public's agenda. Business has the capacity to demonstrate leadership, to model behaviour, and to focus attention on the issues that matter most.

In terms of business returns, there are two reasons why companies should promote their efforts. First, your markets are telling you that they expect you to do good, and they are using their purchasing power to make their point. Second, as in the case of justice, it's not enough for it to be done — it must be *seen* to be done.

People

Your people are your most important strategic resource. Staff at all levels should become involved in your social marketing efforts. It's good for your program, and it's good for company morale and loyalty.

Some companies' employees volunteer at certain events, or more regularly. Other companies have the CEO or senior executives speak about the SMB program. Still other companies extend the program to many internal departments. In all cases, remember that your people can be ambassadors of change.

Policy

It is becoming increasingly common in the Unites States for companies to get involved politically in support of their social marketing programs. For example, Kraft General Foods (U.S.) is lobbying for funding for food stamps as one more effort in its anti-hunger crusade.

While most companies in Canada have yet to take this approach, your program can still be a tool for social action. It can direct people to write letters, contact their representatives, and rally for legislative change. It can educate markets about current policies and necessary reforms. And it can add visibility to the advocacy efforts of your non-profit partner.

Programming Tip #3:

Integration Is Key

Social marketing programs are not just another promotion. Ronald McDonald House has worked because it has become the symbol of the hamburger chain's sustained commitment to kids and families. It is part of the company's core business. It is addressed within the commercial planning cycle. It is heavily promoted. It is renewed and revitalized on a continual basis. It is injected with the imagery and personality normally accorded to brands.

PROGRAM EXTENSION TOOLS
- Include print, video, and audio cassette instructional kits that contain working resources — reproducible fact sheets, artwork, quizzes, print advertisements, etc.
- Build a valuable "multiplier effect" into your program, allowing you to greatly extend your reach within your target populations
- Allow intermediaries to deliver programs to reach your primary social market

RESPONSE/FEEDBACK VEHICLES
- Solicit active response from the target groups
- Include telephone hotlines — individuals can get more information, seek advice, order materials, etc.
- Also include quizzes, questionnaires, and diaries to promote active involvement on the part of individuals
- Can be delivered through print, interactive kiosks, or the Internet

EVENTS
- Often revolve around fund-raising, or around the many days, weeks, and months devoted to specific issues
- Draw both crowds and attention to your issue

SPOKESPEOPLE/CHAMPIONS
- Include people from inside and outside your company (such as celebrities or issue experts)
- Must have credibility and authority with your audiences
- Should be used systematically, i.e., throughout all your media and programming
- Must be informed and well-briefed
- Agree on content with non-profit partners prior to talks with media or other audiences
- Provide briefing books and sample questions for all spokespersons

PROMOTIONS
- Include contests, premiums, cross-promotions, incentives, etc.
- Used as a mechanism for generating funds and promoting awareness

PROMOTIONAL ITEMS
- Include buttons, T-shirts, coasters, key rings, posters, toques, bumper and window stickers, etc., that carry the program slogan, message, or logo
- Help establish a public presence and image for the campaign
- Serve as environmental cues and reminders for behavioural change

SOCIAL PRODUCTS
- Include condoms and needle-cleaning kits — tools for change
- Carefully consider use in SMB program design

Source: Achieving Social Change, Insurance Corporation of British Columbia

What to Do

Choose Your Program Strategy

The social marketing strategy you employ must respond to the particular social needs of your markets. For example, research shows that the onset of smoking is most prevalent among youth aged 12 to 13. Even though these young teens generally know the dangers of smoking, they feel themselves to be invincible. They don't believe that addiction — or death — could possibly happen to them.

For the social marketer trying to deal with smoking, this presents a great problem. Information alone won't work. Strategies based on peer influence, stigmatizing smoking, and creating a social climate intolerant of smoking behaviour are more effective.

Another example: Drinking and driving used to be worn as a badge of honour — the activity was reinforced by a society tolerant of the behaviour. Fortunately, effective anti-drinking and driving campaigns have been successful in stigmatizing this behaviour. Some provinces took it one step further; they decided to reward positive behaviour. Through a partnership between the police and community business, a program was developed where merchandise — such as ice scrapers and license wallets — was given to those individuals who passed spot checks.

For still another program, research showed that teenagers were fearful of raising the subject of condoms with their partners. While they understood the risks of unsafe sex, they lacked the tools to discuss the issue. One effective strategy has been to reduce the stigma attached to condom use. Another has been a skills development approach — provide adolescents with the negotiating tools and techniques they require in order to feel comfortable broaching the subject and managing the exchange.

Create Your Program

Now your task is to create a program that achieves both your social and business objectives. This is a bit of a high wire act. It's easy to lose track of one or the other in the process of program development. Here are a few examples of programs that have managed to adhere to the social agenda and business strategy.

Programming Tip #4:

Location, Location, Location

Geography plays a significant role in your SMB program. Whether your program functions on a national, regional, or local level will depend on a number of factors, including the geography of your target markets and your business units, the issue you've chosen to undertake, and the business goals you've set.

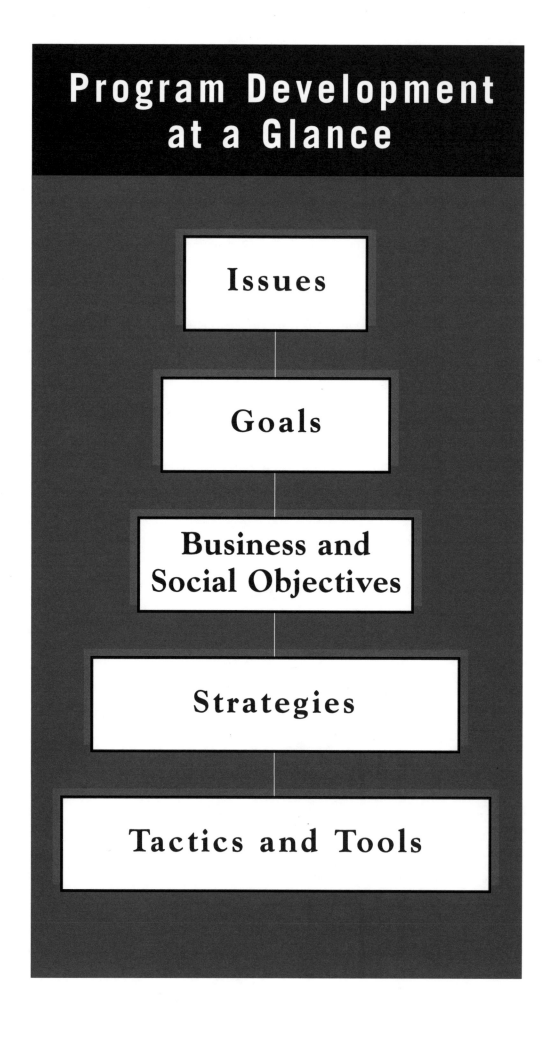

Program Development at a Glance

Issues

Goals

Business and Social Objectives

Strategies

Tactics and Tools

Example #1: A major hotel chain wanted to create a social marketing program that would have social benefit and, at the same time, would achieve a number of business objectives, including:

- customer retention — motivate families to return to the hotel while on the road during summer vacation months

- value to franchisees — a program that would support franchisee marketing and sales efforts

- community profile — a program that would heighten the profile of the hotel within the communities in which it operates

With parents as the primary target market and children as the influencers, the hotel has created a fun and educational program around the issue of road safety. Here's how it works. Upon check-in at the hotel, each child receives a box filled with games and activities focused on road safety rules. The box can be used in the hotel or in the car. The box also contains a guide for parents on rules for the road. Promotions such as contests, on-site gimmicks and cartoon characters brought to life round out the fun part of the program. On a more serious side, the hotel chain is partnering with a major, national non-profit organization dedicated to injury prevention. Part of the initiative is a cause-related marketing effort — the hotel will sell first aid kits, licence plate holders, post cards, etc. with the road safety message — to raise money for the non-profit. Franchisees are provided with programming ideas and tools to extend the program into their communities.

Example #2: Health Canada has developed a guide to help seniors better manage their medication use. The guide has been created in response to an increasingly pressing problem: too many seniors are taking too many prescription and over-the-counter drugs incorrectly, and in wrong combinations.

At the same time, Nissan Canada is taking a leadership role in galvanizing Canadians of all ages to acknowledge and honour the contribution seniors make to our country. With dozens of partnerships with non-profits already in place (e.g., Meals on Wheels) and dealerships nation-wide, Nissan has the distribution system to deliver the guides right to seniors and their caregivers. For Health Canada, the partnership leverages committed dollars. For Nissan, the partnership

Programming Tip #5.

Work Backwards

Consider your timelines. Plan ahead for at least three years. While you may not end up doing a three-year program, it's essential that you have a long-term perspective about change. This kind of orientation will signal to others within your organization that the program is an important and central part of your priority and commitment.

"Long-range planning does not deal with future decisions, but with the future of present decisions."

Peter Drucker

enables the company to provide additional benefit at virtually no extra cost to its primary social market — seniors. The program is promoted through media relations and print advertising in seniors' magazines.

Example #3: Kodak Canada wanted to influence public policy in relation to international competition. Its concern revolved around the uncertain business environment caused by the changing nature of the global marketplace. The company also felt strongly that Canada's private sector had relied too much for too long on government for ideas and solutions to improve competitiveness world-wide. Kodak's call to action? "Industry must take hold of the reins of leadership, both in working with government to explore constructive policies for increasing our competitive position, and in seeking solutions independently amongst ourselves to seize new trading opportunities."

In the context of a multi-year advocacy program, Kodak commissioned research studies and published them in a report entitled *New Visions for Canadian Business…Strategies for competing in the global economy.* The report is designed to generate debate on key issues among government, educators, industry and the technological community. It has become the basis for a series of further studies and reports on related issues.

In all three examples outlined above, a number of principles have been put into practice. First, each program has been designed to establish more meaningful relationships with key markets — whether they be consumers, franchisees or relevant stakeholders. Second, each program is driven by business objectives, but meets social needs. Third, each program capitalizes on distribution systems already in place. Finally, each company has partnered with a relevant non-profit organization to ensure issue accuracy and credibility.

Promote Your Program

Promoting your SMB program is a matter of choosing the right social marketing vehicles, and of delivering the messages that will motivate and sustain behavior change.

In selecting your vehicles, you'll probably use many of the same tools you use now to market your products and services. Understanding the strengths and limitations of vehicles in terms of their ability to influence target groups is, of course, essential (refer to pages 76 and 78 for a list of these programming options).

Programming Tip #6:

Consider Your Assets.

SMB programs cost money, but often, they can be built around existing assets. As you develop your program, think about the distribution systems, the media access, and the infrastructure you have at your disposal.

Developing Your Program

WHAT TO KNOW

➻ **How People Change**
Know social learning theory

➻ **The Six Ps of the Social Marketing Mix**

1	**PRODUCT**	Know your program objectives
2	**PLACE**	Know your distribution channels
3	**PRICE**	Know the risks and benefits of charging
4	**PROMOTION**	Know the power of marketing ideas
5	**PEOPLE**	Know the strength of this strategic resource
6	**POLICY**	Know your advocacy role

WHAT TO DO

➻ **Choose your program strategy**
Base it on social change theory

➻ **Create your program**
Make it long-term and multi-faceted

➻ **Promote your program**
Develop the right messages for
the right people

➻ **Schedule it**
Launch at the right time

It is also important that vehicles be integrated and orchestrated for maximum effect. As with product marketing, one-shot efforts won't succeed. You need reach, frequency and impact. You need to invest the dollars necessary in order to see the return you're after.

Determining how to frame and present your social change messages is a little more tricky. While SMB has much in common with commercial marketing techniques, one area of difference is the social message. It's vital to remember that you are not selling a product — you are generating buy-in to an idea or practice.

The commercial marketplace strives to create messages that shock or grab attention. Social marketers also want to draw attention to their messages, but the techniques are somewhat different. For example, the latest thinking in the field says that "body bag" commercials, or "This is Your Brain on Drugs" ads, inspire fear but do little to change behaviour (see pages 72 and 74). On another front, there is a growing understanding among the international development education community that fund-raising appeals based on perpetual crises and images of poverty, famine, tragedy, and death may work in the short term, but ultimately result in audience apathy and neglect. And, some ads just plain offend. A prime example is Benetton's AIDS campaign, a program that seems to have more shock value than social value.

For your creative to be effective, it needs to take into account the dynamics of social change and the triggers that will motivate people to take action. Information alone, no matter how devastating (e.g., "This many children die unnecessarily each year because of this or that"), will not generally change behaviour. Theories of attitude and behaviour change must be understood and used as a basis for creative efforts.

Schedule It

Your social agenda should be linked to your business strategy. When is the most opportune time to launch your program? Should it be done in conjunction with a product launch? A store opening? A special event? Should it stand on its own and be used as a means of generating coverage during those times when you're not engaged in an active launch or promotion? Just as there are opportune times to introduce new products into the marketplace, so too is there a social schedule. If you are launching an arts program, for example, it may be wise to avoid Arts Awareness Week, when your messages could get lost in the clamour of competition.

Programming Tip #7:

Buying vs. Buying-in

While SMB has much in common with commercial marketing techniques, one area of difference is the social message. It's vital to remember that you are not selling a product — you are generating buy-in to an idea or practice. That means you've got to base your creative strategies not on consumer principles, but on theories of social attitude and behavior change.

TURNING PLANS INTO ACTION

The map is not the territory

t this point in the process, you should have a strategy and program plan that serves as a blueprint for action over the next few years.

Implementing your program will be challenging. SMB presents new ways of thinking and new ways of doing business. It involves creating new kinds of relationships with markets. It calls for true collaboration with your non-profit or government partner. It means dealing with a whole new set of audiences — social markets, intermediaries, influencers — that have different priorities and ways of operating. It requires you to understand not only how to market products, but how to promote issues and ideas. And keep in mind that you probably won't have tangible results to show in your first year.

That is why your implementation strategy is paramount. Your ideas may be first-rate, but they won't have the impact you're after unless their execution is carefully and strategically designed.

The cornerstone of successful implementation is locating your SMB program in the business agenda. It is essential that it be part of mainstream planning and programming, central to business objectives, and a clear manifestation of your corporate values.

The cornerstone of successful implementation is locating your SMB program in the business agenda. It is essential that it be part of mainstream planning and programming, central to business objectives, and a clear manifestation of your corporate values.

What to Know

SMB Goes Beyond Principle

The credibility and centrality of SMB originate from the inside. Good intentions will not likely generate much argument, but buy-in and commitment will only result from moving from principle to practice. Internal markets will only make SMB a priority if it meets their needs, and if it is perceived as a means to their ends. If your SMB program does not help employees meet their goals, then it will remain a marginalized effort, both in your own department and throughout the company.

Leadership Is Essential

Because senior decision-makers are key in establishing credibility and profile for your SMB program, it is important that they see its merits and that it becomes integral to their thinking. Top company officials, including your CEO, should demonstrate commitment to the principles of the program through visible initiatives both inside and outside the company.

Year 1: An SMB Agenda

You've conducted your research and developed your SMB program. Now it's time to turn strategy into action. What you do in the program's first year of existence will determine its success or failure in the long term. Here are some steps you can take to help ensure an effective implementation process.

INSIDE

1. Create a task force that includes representatives from relevant departments

2. Get input from the task force about the program and refine it accordingly

3. Sell the SMB program to top management, other departments, and internal markets

4. Recruit key senior management to support and promote the program

5. Launch a communication program to promote the SMB concept

6. Keep internal audiences informed about relevant action and, where feasible, early success stories

OUTSIDE

1. Launch the SMB Big Idea through a promotional program

2. Create highly visible events or programs that attract media and market attention and enable internal audiences to participate

3. Monitor and evaluate activity and impact

Partnership Starts at Home

Presumably, you've already decided on the author of the program: a brand, a product line, the corporate entity, or your company's foundation. Wherever the program is housed, make sure it becomes a central priority within that department; it should not be marginalized through lack of focus or attention.

The program should also be extended to other departments within the company so that resources are leveraged to maximum effect and synergies are realized. SMB's potential for delivering value across the company should be clearly demonstrated. In other words, showcase how SMB can help others meet their goals and objectives.

Your SMB program should be extended to other departments within the company so that resources are leveraged to maximum effect and synergies are realized.

If, for example, your program resides in public affairs, then it would make sense to involve marketing, human resources, perhaps research and development. Let's say that your company is a bank and your issue is numeracy. While your program may be primarily focused on educating the public about the need for and value of competency with numbers, your human resources department may want to create a program to help your staff, their spouses, or their children develop their math skills. Involve marketing by creating a promotion or contest around certain products that can be delivered through the branches.

Early Success Matters

Early success is essential to success down the road. The difficulty, however, is that program results are not generally evident early on. It's hard to demonstrate success if there's not much to talk about.

Early success depends, in large part, on visibility of commitment. The key is to galvanize and mobilize the troops around ideas, initiatives, and action. Your goal is to generate support and buy-in across the company by creating highly visible programs that staff can participate in or feel proud of. Examples of such programming include events (e.g., walk-a-thons, awareness days, etc.), a cause-related marketing program to raise funds for your non-profit partner, or well-publicized speaking engagements by your CEO or other senior staff.

Time Is of the Essence

Your Social Marketing for Business program must be on the table during the company's regular planning cycle. In this way, it becomes integral to core decision-making and will be assessed for its value and

7 Reasons Why SMB Programs Don't Happen or Don't Work

1. The SMB initiative has not secured corporate-wide commitment

2. Sufficient resources have not been allocated to the program

3. The SMB program has no home — no department to which it belongs, and no single person or group accountable for its success or failure

4. The program does not have a champion to sell and promote it internally

5. The program has little perceived benefit among key departments and senior company officials

6. Measurements are not appropriate; the result is that the program is evaluated based on the wrong criteria

7. The program does not meet the needs of the company's systems — employees, retailers, dealers, distributors, etc.

merit each step of the way. While the danger is that the SMB program can get cut, the upside is that if it does survive, it will enjoy the appropriate level of attention and priority.

Money Is Commitment

There's no way around it — SMB programs cost money. They require the same level of financial commitment as other marketing activities. The good news is that you may not necessarily need to allocate new money. Re-deploying your own budgets, and tying into the budgets of others, may be possible.

Look not only at costs, but also at returns. SMB programs should be judged on their potential to deliver value. And, consider the cost of not undertaking an SMB program. As Philip Kotler states, "Companies pay too much attention to the cost of doing something. They should worry more about the cost of not doing it." In other words, don't forget to take into account opportunity cost. Can you afford *not* to establish more meaningful relationships with your markets by responding to their social concerns? Can you afford *not* to find innovative ways to differentiate yourself and build equity?

Suppliers Must Be Considered

Your suppliers probably include advertising agencies, direct-mail houses, promotional companies, and public relations firms. Likely, they are all experts in their fields of business. But that doesn't necessarily mean they're also experts in social marketing. It's important that you understand your suppliers' capabilities.

That's not to say that your suppliers can't be an integral part of your SMB development team. But don't expect that because they can market products or services, they can market social ideas and issues just as well. Don't expect them to know the politics and sensitivities of the non-profit and government sectors. Don't expect, for example, that promotion houses will know right from the start how to meaningfully integrate a social issue into their repertoire. Attaching your corporate identity to a sporting event or contest is fundamentally different from aligning yourself with a social issue. As discussed earlier, you'll need to know the players, the social marketplace, and the social theories that underlie message and program strategy. This is a relatively new area for most companies, and most agencies.

"Companies pay too much attention to the cost of doing something. They should worry more about the cost of not doing it."

Philip Kotler

The SMB Program Task Force

The following provides a list of those departments that should be represented on your SMB Program Task Force.

Department	What They Bring
Public Affairs	• Management of corporate image • Management of public, media, and government relations • Production of corporate communication: annual report, brochures, advertising, etc. • Issue and crisis management
Marketing	• Understanding of consumer markets • Responsibility for brand image • Control of advertising/promotion
Sales	• Relationships with trade • Knowledge of sales marketplace
Donations	• Knowledge of donation request trends • Management of corporate giving policy and program
Operations	• Responsibility for mechanics of production and distribution • Relationship with suppliers
Research and Development	• Responsibility for product/service development and improvement • Knowledge of current and future capabilities of company in terms of product/service change
Human Resources	• Direct access to all employees • Knowledge of employees' interests, attitudes, and concerns • Responsibility for professional development and training

What to Do

Market Social Marketing

To generate support for your program internally, you've got to start selling. Sell up, down, and across. Start with senior executives and work your way up to the CEO. Outline how the upper echelon can be involved. Then focus your efforts on other departments. Deliver detailed presentations that demonstrate the value the program can have for each department. Offer program ideas that respond to departments' challenges and priorities for the year and beyond. In selling the program, remember that internal markets are people with needs. Position your SMB program as a potential solution to their problems. If you can't find a way to make your program make sense to others, there's probably something wrong with it.

If you can't find a way to make your program make sense to others, there's probably something wrong with it.

Create a Task Force

No matter what department you're in, don't undertake an SMB program without the input and participation of others. One option is to create an interdisciplinary task force composed of representatives from relevant departments. The task force can be initiated after you've completed your program strategy. Its purpose is to help refine, sell, and promote the SMB initiative. Such a task force has a number of benefits:

- It enables you to generate a certain level of buy-in right from the start. This won't address all your internal support issues, but it will be a big help.

- It can alert you to early signs of trouble. The broader your base of representatives, the more you'll know how others in the company perceive your ideas.

- Members of your task force will become departmental champions, so you don't have to do all the work yourself.

- It allows you to share the spoils — once the initiative begins generating results, those involved in the early stages will reap the rewards of being associated with a program that works.

Sequence

Presumably, your action plan lays out all the initiatives you're going to undertake over the next three years. But what comes first? How should activities be sequenced for maximum business and social impact? In other words, what happens when?

In Review

Turning Programs into Action

WHAT TO KNOW

- **SMB Goes Beyond Principle**
  Know needs and priorities
- **Leadership Is Essential**
  Know whose endorsement counts
- **Partnership Starts at Home**
  Know who to include
- **Early Success Matters**
  Know how to mobilize the troops
- **Time Is of the Essence**
  Know your cycles
- **Money Is Commitment**
  Know how to allocate
- **Suppliers Must be Considered**
  Know their strengths and weaknesses

WHAT TO DO

- **Market Social Marketing**
  Sell up, down, and across
- **Create a Task Force**
  Share the work and the spoils
- **Sequence**
  Implement for maximum impact
- **Showcase the Big Idea**
  Market your SMB intent
- **Evaluate Against Criteria**
  Measure success from the start

Sequencing is somewhat complicated because there are two issues to keep in mind. From a business point of view, you have to consider how your program will build corporate or brand equity over time. From a social perspective, you have to determine when target groups need to be reached with the messages and programs that will influence their attitudes and behaviours. What this means, then, is that you've got an added component to consider in designing your implementation plan.

The first year should be dedicated, in large part, to marketing the SMB program as a whole.

Showcase the Big Idea

The first year should be dedicated, in large part, to marketing your SMB program as a whole. In other words, market the concept upon which you're going to hang individual initiatives. Doing so provides a context for promoting mutually reinforcing programs and, ultimately, for ensuring that efforts add up to more than the sum of their parts.

The Big Idea, or your SMB agenda, is your first social marketing product, and marketing it is your most important demonstration of commitment — both inside the company and out. Package and promote it by creating a "manifesto" (or vision document), by securing speaking engagements for your top people, by undertaking media relations around the program, and by marketing it internally.

Evaluate Against Criteria

Finally, as we discussed in Chapter 2, "Defining Success," it is essential that you measure success right from the start. Here, once again, are three key principles to keep in mind:

- Evaluate the right things at the right time. There's no point in measuring increase in sales in the first six months. But it's probably a good idea to test employee response and commitment to the SMB program in that time frame.

- Count whatever is countable. It may seem futile, for example, to count how much support you've generated around the program. Just the opposite is true. The more consensus and buy-in to the program, the better able you'll be to sell the program through the system.

- Don't compare apples and oranges. Don't let your SMB program take the blame for problems it is not responsible for.

THE FINAL
ANALYSIS

I n the final analysis, the effectiveness of your SMB program will be a function of three factors: the level of priority you give social activism on your business agenda; the diligence you apply to developing your SMB strategy; and, the discipline with which you execute it.

Together, the seven principles of Social Marketing for Business presented here provide a framework for a sound planning process. Having now been through it from beginning to end, you are in a position to make some hard-nosed business decisions:

- Does your business need to re-think and re-tool its approach to social action?

- Is SMB the means to your business and social ends?

- Can you generate the internal commitment required to translate your SMB plan into action?

The fact that you find yourself asking such questions is an indication of how much things have changed. Five years ago, if someone tried to tell you that doing well in the marketplace would soon depend on doing good in the world, you probably would have dismissed such a notion as irrelevant. Today, doing good is approaching the status of a basic business management skill. Five years from now, whether or not your company has an effective SMB program will likely be a key determinant of the health of your bottom line.

SOURCES

Arnott, Nancy. "Marketing With a Passion." *Sales & Marketing Management*, January, 1994.

"Avon Fights Back Against Cancer." *Cosmetics*, March, 1994.

Beale, Nigel. "HMV Promo Rooted in Savvy Marketing." *Strategy*, November 28, 1994.

Behar, Richard. "They Gave Too Much." *Forbes 400*, October 1, 1984.

Brown, Louise. "It All Ads Up." *Starweek*, April 4, 1995.

"Canadian Firms Learning How to Do Well by Doing Good." *The Toronto Star*, March 27, 1989.

Cannon, Margaret. "Doing Well by Doing Good." *Canadian Business*, March, 1987.

Carroll, Ginny. "Getting with the Cleanup." *Newsweek*, September 25, 1989.

"Caught in the Crossfire." *Corporate Philanthropy Report*, April, 1986.

"Charity at Work." *Maclean's*, January 11, 1993.

Cohen, Andrew. "Corporate Giving Remains Too Small a Part of Business." *The Financial Post 500*, Summer, 1987.

Cook, Dan. "Nothing Sells Like Sports." *Business Week*, August 31, 1987.

Cone/Roper. *"Benchmark Survey on Cause-Related Marketing."* December, 1993.

Crane, David. "Business Must Look Beyond Profit." *The Toronto Star*, November 15, 1994.

Crawford, Michael. "The Law and the Jungle." *Canadian Business*, February, 1992.

Crawford, Purdy. "An Incubator Project for Small Businesses." *Canadian Business Review*, Autumn, 1991.

Cross, Richard and Janet Smith. *"Customer Bonding. Pathway to Lasting Customer Loyalty."* Chicago, Illinois: NTC Business Books, 1995.

Drumwright, Minette. "Socially Responsible Organizational Buying: Environmental Concern as a Noneconomic Buying Criterion." *Journal of Marketing*, July, 1994.

D'Cruz, Joseph and Alan Rugman. "New Visions for Canadian Business...Strategies for competing in the global economy." *Faculty of Management, University of Toronto*, 1990.

Entine, Jon. "Rain-forest Chic." *Report on Business Magazine*, October, 1995.

Fowlie, Laura. "Fostering Innovation in Gift-Giving." *The Financial Post*, December 09, 1994.

Furlong, Carla. "Government 'Hands Out." *BCB*, February, 1995.

Habib, Marlene. "Roots Founders Support Group that Aids Kids." *The Toronto Star*, September 28, 1995.

Henkoff, Ronald. "Is Greed Dead?" *Fortune*, August 14, 1989.

Holman, Blan and Ned Martel. "Inside the Environmental Groups, 1994." *Outside*, March, 1994.

Huntley, Helen. "More Charities Look to Business for Help." *St. Petersburg Times*, April 1, 1991.

Hurson, Tim. "Social Marketing: The Competitive Edge." Speech delivered to the Canadian Society of Association Executives, 1994.

Kapstein, Jonathan, and Micheal Schroeder. "Charity Doesn't Begin at Home Anymore." *Business Week*, February 25, 1991.

Kindel, Stephen. "America's Band." *Forbes*, January 30, 1984.

Kotler, Philip. *"Marketing for Non-Profit Organizations, 2nd Edition."* Englewood Cliffs, New Jersey: Prentice-Hall, Inc., 1982.

Labich, Kenneth. "Kissing Off Corporate America." *Fortune*, February 20, 1995.

Levine, Joshua. "I Gave at the Supermarket." *Forbes*, December 25, 1989.

Mehr, Martin. "Sponsorship: A New Marketing Arena." *Marketing*, June 6, 1988.

Menzies, David. "Wearing a Cause on Your Corporate Sleeve." *Food in Canada*, November/December, 1994.

"All for a Good Cause." *Marketing*, September 26, 1994.

Mickleburgh, Rod. "Avon Says Cancer Campaign Could Help Patient Groups." *The Globe and Mail*, November 19, 1993.

Miller, Cyndee. "Sexy Sizzle Backfires." *Marketing News*, September 25, 1995.

"Molson Marketing Recognized for Excellence." *AdNews On-Line Daily*, October 6, 1995.

Moore, Sean. "Corporate World's Time for Shelling Out Has Come." *The Globe & Mail*, August 24, 1989.

Murphy, Anne. "The Seven (Almost) Deadly Sins of High Minded Entrepreneurs." *Inc.*, July 1994.

Nathanson, Janice. "Lending a Helping Hand." *Association Magazine*, January, 1995.

Nitkan, David. "Structural Changes in Canadian Corporate Philanthropy." *Corporate Ethics Monitor Volume 7. Issue 3*, May-June, 1995.

Oldenburg, Dan. "Socially Correct Marketing." *The Washington Post*, March 7, 1994.

Ono, Yumiko. "Advertisers Try 'Doing Good' to Help Make Sales Do Better." *The Wall Street Journal*, September 2, 1994.

Pope, Bruce. Speech delivered at the 1995 Sales and Marketing Executives International Excellence in Marketing Awards. 1995.

Powell, Johanna. "Charities Seek Partnerships to Raise Money." *The Financial Post*, December 9, 1994.

Powell, Johanna. "Star Athletes Raise Awareness, Cash for Cystic Fibrosis." *The Financial Post*, December 9, 1994.

Riehl, Gordon. "Charity May Pay Off for Corporations." *The Globe and Mail*, March 28, 1988.

Sarner, Mark. "Marketing Health to Canadians." *Health Promotion Magazine*, 1984.

Sarner, Mark. "Social Marketing: The New Marketing Imperative." Speech delivered at *Doing Well, Doing Good* conference, October, 1994.

Sarner, Mark. "Social Marketing and the New Philanthropy." Presentation to the Institute for Donations and Public Affairs Research, 1995.

Sarner, Mark. "Adding Values: The Next Marketing Frontier." Speech delivered to the annual meeting of the Canadian Soft Drink Association.

Scotland, Randall. "Canadian Airlines Takes Unicef Under Its Wing." *The Financial Post*, November 29, 1994.

Scott, Kenneth. "Social Marketing Must Be More than Lip Service." *The Sponsorship Report*, November 1994.

Smith, Craig. "The New Corporate Philanthropy." *Harvard Business Review*, May/June 1994.

Smith, Geoffrey, and Ron Stodghill II. "Are Good Causes Good Marketing?" *Marketing*, March 21, 1994.

Smith, Vivian. "Breast-Cancer Politics Tangles Avon Campaign." *The Globe and Mail*, November 13, 1995.

Stevenson, Mark. "What's in It for Me?" *Marketing*, December 1993.

Strauss, Marina. "Body Shop's Success Fuels its Competition." *The Globe and Mail*, October 20, 1994.

Stultz, Janice E. "The Decision to Give: Methods and Rewards of Corporate Philanthropy." *Directors & Boards*, Winter 1980.

Sullivan, Michael. "Rethinking Corporate Philanthropy in the 1990s." *Decima Research*, 1991.

Summerfield, Patty. "Allying for the Public Good." *Marketing*, February 13, 1989.

Taylor, Allan R. "What's your Company's Community Contribution." *Commercial News*, February 1990.

"The Chivas Regal Report on Working Americans: Emerging Values for the 1990s." *Research and Forecasts*, 1989.

Trachtenberg, Jeffery A. "Beyond the 30-second Spot." *Forbes*, December 17, 1984

Vale, Norma. "All for a Good Cause." *Front & Centre*, March 1995.

Valpy, Michael. "Ways to Harness a Community's Assets." *The Globe and Mail*, September 28, 1995.

Vartorella, William F. "An Insider's Guide to Getting Equipment Grants." *Nonprofit Management Strategies*, October, 1992.

Wallach, Van. "Matters of Survival." *Advertising Age*, November 9, 1988.

Wallis, Brian. "The Art of Big Business." *Art in America*, June 1986.

Wellemeyer, Marilyn. "The Joys of Closeup Philanthropy." *Fortune*, September 1, 1986.

White, Greg. *The Market Vision 2000 Study*. 1992.

Young, Eric and Mitchell Temkin. *Achieving Social Change: Insurance Corporation of British Columbia*, 1991.

NOTES

NOTES